Wikis for School Leaders

Using Technology to Improve Communication and Collaboration

Stephanie D. Sandifer

Eye On Education
6 Depot Way West, Suite 106
Larchmont, NY 10538
(914) 833-0551
(914) 833-0761 fax
www.eyeoneducation.com

Copyright © 2011 Eye On Education, Inc.
All Rights Reserved.

For information about permission to reproduce selections from this book, write: Eye On Education, Permissions Dept., Suite 106, 6 Depot Way West, Larchmont, NY 10538

Portions of this book previously appeared in Stephanie D. Sandifer's *Wikified Schools: Using Wikis to Improve Communication and Collaboration in Education* (Wakefield Publishing, 2009).

Library of Congress Cataloging-in-Publication Data

Sandifer, Stephanie D.
  Wikis for school leaders : using technology to improve communication and collaboration/Stephanie D. Sandifer.
       p.   cm.
  Includes bibliographical references.
  ISBN 978-1-59667-184-3
  1. School management and organization—Technological innovations.
  2. School administrators—Professional relationships.
  3. Communication in education.
  4. Wikis (Computer science)
  I. Title.
  LB2806.17.S26 2011
  371.2—dc22   2011006796

10 9 8 7 6 5 4 3 2 1

Sponsoring Editor: Robert Sickles
Production Editor: Lauren Beebe
Copyeditor: Carol Rawleigh
Designer and Compositor: Matthew Williams
Cover Designer: Dave Strauss

Also Available from Eye On Education

Leading School Change:
9 Strategies to Bring *Everybody* On Board
Todd Whitaker

Get Organized!
Time Management for School Leaders
Frank Buck

Classroom Walkthroughs to Improve Teaching and Learning
Donald Kachur, Judy Stout, and Claudia Edwards

Problem-Solving Tools & Tips for School Leaders
Cathie E. West

The Principalship from A to Z
Ronald Williamson and Barbara R. Blackburn

Rigorous Schools and Classrooms: Leading the Way
Ronald Williamson and Barbara R. Blackburn

Rigor in Your School: A Toolkit for Leaders
Ronald Williamson and Barbara R. Blackburn

Professional Learning Communities:
An Implementation Guide and Toolkit
Kathleen A. Foord and Jean M. Haar

Professional Development: What Works
Sally J. Zepeda

Motivating & Inspiring Teachers, Second Edition
Todd Whitaker, Beth Whitaker, and Dale Lumpa

Creating School Cultures that Embrace Learning:
What Successful Leaders Do
Tony Thacker, John S. Bell, and Franklin P. Schargel

Differentiation Is an *Expectation*:
A School Leader's Guide to Building a Culture of Differentiation
Kimberly Hewitt and Daniel Weckstein

Executive Skills for Busy School Leaders
Chris Hitch and David Coley

For Clare, Austin, Dillan, and Payton.

About the Author

Stephanie Sandifer is the author of the Change Agency blog, an online educator, and a consultant who lives and works in Houston, Texas. She is an experienced educator whose background includes teaching high school and college-level courses in studio art, design, computer graphics, animation, and research methods. She has also provided instructional leadership at the campus and district levels as a School Improvement Facilitator, Dean of Instruction, Small Learning Community Coordinator, Curriculum Specialist, and Literacy Coach. Throughout her career in education she has constantly advocated for technology integration across the curriculum. She consults and presents workshops regionally and nationally on topics ranging from technology integration, Web 2.0, effective instructional strategies, and school improvement.

Author's Website: http://stephaniesandifer.com
Change Agency blog: http://ed421.com
Wikified Schools: http://wikifiedschools.com

Acknowledgments

This book could not have been written without the "critical friendship" of many people. I want to first thank my entire online Personal Learning Network (PLN)—hundreds of people with whom I connect, collaborate, and learn on a daily basis. Through our shared learning and our challenging conversations I have gained the knowledge and skill to make this book possible. I am unable to list all of these people here—you know who you are because we connect on our blogs, through Twitter, on one of many wikis or Ning networks, or through Facebook.

I also want to thank my former and current colleagues who have been willing to try this "new thing" called a wiki, and who have challenged me and supported my interest in pushing the envelope in order to improve the quality of our work together. On a similar note, I want to thank everyone who has been a part of my learning experience around school improvement, including the staff of Houston A+ Challenge. Their support and guidance across multiple initiatives has been incredibly valuable to me.

Additionally, the ideas in this book have evolved and have been expanded through numerous discussions with so many participants and attendees at my workshops and presentations. While others are learning from me, I have also been learning from them.

I am also very grateful for the guidance and hard work on the part of everyone at Eye On Education who was involved with bringing this work to print.

Finally, and most importantly, I want to thank my family—my parents, my partner, and my children especially—for so much unconditional love and support. Thank you for all that you do and all that you are to me.

Table of Contents

About the Author vii
Acknowledgments ix
Table of Contents xi
Free Downloads xv
Online Resources xv
Introduction xvii

1 **Organization and Collaboration in the B.W. (Before Wiki) Era** 1

2 **What Is A Wiki?** 5
   Public Wikis vs. Enterprise Wikis 6
   Wikis, Google Docs, and Blogs—What's the Difference? 6

3 **Why Use A Wiki?** 9
   A Paradigm Shift 9
   The Wiki Future Is Now 17
   Reflection Questions 19

4 **When & Where?** 21
   Wikis for Leadership and Administration 21
   Communication and Knowledge Management 23
   Building Action Plans 25
   Transform Meetings 26
   Personal Portfolios 29
   Wikis for Professional Learning and Faculty Collaboration 31
         Professional Learning Communities 31
         Critical Friends Groups 33
         Other Team Collaboration Ideas 34
         Lesson Plans 35
         Curriculum Mapping 35
   Professional Development 37
         Site-Based Professional Development 37
   Wikis for Home-to-School Communications and Collaboration 40
   Wikis in the Classroom 43
   Student Voice and Leadership 46
   Security Issues 48
   Reflection Questions 49

5   How?—Making It Work in Your Organization 51
- Dos & Don'ts 53
- Getting Started 56
- Technology Coach 62
- Logistics and Use of Specific Wikis 63
- BASICS: The Anatomy of a Wiki 67
  - Article or Content Page 67
  - Discussion Page 68
  - Revision History 70
  - The Importance of Tagging 72
  - Edit or Page Notes 73
  - Links 74
- Wiki Etiquette 74
- Reflection Questions 76

6   Sustaining Wikis 77

7   Web 2.0 Tools That Support Wiki Use 83
- Google Docs 83
- Google Spreadsheets and Forms 84
- Google Presentations 84
- Blogs 88
- Twitter 88
- Social Networking 89
- Social Bookmarking 89
- RSS Feed Aggregators 90
- Live Broadcasting and Web Conferencing 91

8   Wiki Continued—Edit This Chapter 93

Resources for Successful Wiki Use 95
- PBWorks Syntax 97
- Wikispaces Syntax 98
- WetPaint Syntax 99
- MediaWiki Syntax 100
- Wiki Adoption Action Plan 101
- Wiki Introduction—Sample Workshop Agenda 102
- Wiki Scavenger Hunt 105
- Wiki Barn Raising—Personal Profiles 106
  - Before The Session 106
  - Protocol 106
- Agenda for Short Introduction to Wiki Session 107
  - Links 109
  - Wiki Examples 109

Wiki Workshop Workbook..110
    Instructions:...110
    Notes...110

Habit Building Guide 111
Teacher 2.0/Administrator 2.0 One Step at a Time:
    A Week-by-Week Guide to Building Web 2.0 Habits............113
    Suggestions for Use of This Guide.............................114
Getting Started: Computer and Web Browser.......................115
    Instruction & Task..115
    Reflection Questions..116
RSS & Aggregators: Create an Account and Subscribe to the Web 117
    Instruction & Task..117
        Your task is:...117
    Tips for Habit Building.......................................118
    Reflection Questions..119
Organizing Your Feeds..120
    Instruction & Task..120
    Tips for Habit Building.......................................121
    Reflection Questions..121
Share Your Subscriptions..122
    Instruction & Task..122
    Tips for Habit Building.......................................123
    Reflection Questions..123
Creating Your iGoogle Home Page.................................124
    Instruction & Task..124
    Tips for Habit Building.......................................124
    Reflection Questions:...125
Blog Reading 126
    Instruction & Task..126
    Tips for Habit Building.......................................126
    Reflection Questions..127
Wikifying Your Work 128
    Instruction & Task..128
    Tips for Habit Building.......................................128
    Reflection Questions..129

Glossary 131
Recommended Resources 133
References...137

Free Downloads

Select materials in this book are also available on Eye On Education's website as Adobe Acrobat files. Permission has been granted to purchasers of this book to download these materials and print them.

You can access these downloads by visiting Eye On Education's website: www.eyeoneducation.com. From the home page, click on FREE, then click on Supplemental Downloads. Alternatively, you can search or browse our website to find this book, then click on "Log in to Access Supplemental Downloads."

Your book-buyer access code is **WSL-7184-3**.

Index of Free Downloads
Habit Building Guide 111–130
    Teacher 2.0/Administrator 2.0 One Step at a Time:
        A Week-by-Week Guide to Building Web 2.0 Habits. 113
    Getting Started: Computer and Web Browser. 115
    RSS & Aggregators: Create an Account and Subscribe to the Web 117
    Organizing Your Feeds 120
    Share Your Subscriptions 122
    Creating Your iGoogle Home Page. 124
    Blog Reading 126
    Wikifying Your Work 128

Online Resources

This book offers readers several online resources for further research, supplemental materials, and user involvement. For ease of access, these links have been posted on Wikified Schools (**http://wikifiedschools.com**) and on the book's product page on Eye On Education's website (**www.eyeoneducation.com**). From the home page, search by author or book title to locate the *Wikis for School Leaders* page. Then scroll to the bottom of the page and click on **Online Resources** for an index of easily clickable links.

Introduction

This book is about change—the change that occurs when we use a powerful web-based technology to achieve effective and efficient collaboration, creativity, and communication. This book is about technology, but it is also about best practice. How do we leverage technology—specifically wikis and other web-based tools—to improve our collaboration, creative thinking, communication, problem solving, and change processes? How do we make better use of our time and better use of technology resources such as server space and email? How do we model 21st century tools for better communication and collaboration across all levels of our educational organizations?

Communication and collaboration in a school environment can be very challenging. Education leaders face a variety of difficulties when trying to implement new programs and new initiatives. Teachers may often feel as if they get conflicting or inadequate information from school or district leadership, and they may feel the urge to resist change by shutting the classroom door. Educators who work at the district office on collaborative teams often rely extensively on effective communication and collaboration among the members to produce curriculum and instructional products that must be shared with campuses to improve practice at the campus level. Indeed, everyone at all levels in the system face many challenges in effective and efficient communication and collaboration.

However, all educators at every level do have the best intentions and quite often the problem is not an intentional lapse in communication, but rather ineffective methods of communication. In my work with school reform I have come to the conclusion that one of our biggest challenges in school improvement at any level is communication (or the lack thereof) followed closely by ineffective collaboration. Prior to my experience with Web 2.0 technologies, I frequently searched for more effective ways of working with my team members and better ways of communicating with individuals as well as with groups of teachers and administrators. As I began exploring the world of Web 2.0, I finally stumbled across tools that made it much easier to achieve my goals and to be much more productive. The most powerful of all of these new tools is the wiki.

I know firsthand how difficult it can be to coach adults in the use of new tools and how challenging it can be to roll out new technology. In my years of providing training and support to other teachers and administrators who need help with new technology, I have worked with a variety of teams focused on developing effective training and support programs. The lessons learned through all of those training, coaching, and support experiences are applied in my approach to implementing wikis across a school or district.

Before we begin discussing the what, so what, and now what of wiki use and adoption, let me provide a warning: Wikis are not silver bullets. There is no promise made anywhere in this book that wiki adoption will be easy or pain-free in your organization, or that it will solve all of your problems. Faculty and staff are accustomed to many other ways of working—even though those ways may not be the most effective or efficient in achieving the outcomes desired by the organization. You will be moving their cheese. They will resist. Therefore, you and everyone else involved in moving forward with wiki adoption must remain persistent in your efforts. After three and a half years of promoting wiki use within my district, it is only recently that I have seen the momentum begin to shift as more teams and campuses have started to create their own wikis. This shift has been long and hard with more than one failed attempt at wiki adoption. However, each failure also provided valuable lessons—lessons which will be shared throughout this book. No change is ever easy and the status quo can be a stubborn opponent. The success of wiki adoption in your organization will depend heavily on the leadership at all levels within your organization. Technology alone does not create a utopia.

We will also explore a few other Web 2.0 tools that incorporate some wiki-like features and offer more opportunities for improved communication and collaboration. Fortunately, new tools are constantly emerging that make use of the best features of wikis, giving educators the potential to work evermore effectively and efficiently. A "wikified school" will make use of any and all technology tools that increase productivity and allow the educators to focus on student learning. However, becoming a wikified school is about so much more than just adopting the right technology. This is a paradigm shift to a much flatter (as opposed to a hierarchical) work environment where the faculty and staff become more empowered to initiate and contribute to significant change across the entire organization. This paradigm shift—enabled by these technologies—provides opportunities for all stakeholders to have a much larger voice in planning, decision making, and leadership.

Finally, and most important, this book is about learning. As educators—as learning professionals—our work *is* learning. We are tasked with facilitating the learning of others, but also of facilitating our own learning. It is my firm belief that everything that is done in a school and within a school district should be focused on what is best for the students and not on what is easiest or most comfortable for the adults. The use of a wiki should result in better use of time, improved communication, and increased adult learning, which in turn will contribute to improved student learning. Ward Cunningham, the developer of the very first wiki software, once described the wiki as "The simplest thing that could possibly work" (Venners, 2004). However, the initial use of a wiki will not be comfortable or easy for adults who are not familiar with it. It is easy to avoid changing practice when "the old way" is more comfortable, even when the old way is less efficient and less effective.

Educators want to be viewed as skilled professionals, yet are more likely to prefer being competent at the old wrong thing than incompetent at the new right thing (Black and Gregersen, 2002). In order to improve student learning, we must be model learners. We must be lead learners. We must be willing to take risks and to risk being uncomfortable as we learn new ways of working. So step out of your comfort zone and join me as we explore the use of wikis in our work.

1
Organization and Collaboration in the B.W. (Before Wiki) Era

"To succeed in this new world, it will not be enough—indeed, it will be counterproductive—simply to intensify current policies, management strategies, and curricular approaches."
—Tapscott and Williams

Ask any educator what his or her "core mission" is and most will respond with something along the lines of "education" or "learning" or "success for all students." Most of our schools and our school districts include this language in their mission statements. Ask any educator what his or her number one priority is in daily responsibilities, and the response will usually relate to the mission of "education for all." This is a noble mission to undertake, and many educators find it to be a most challenging task. The business of educating learners has become more complex over the past century, and our school systems have responded by adding more layers of everything from curriculum standards and policies, management and bureaucracy, to school structures and state and federal laws. The traditional approach to managing all these elements has been a hierarchical structure rooted in early 20th century management theory pioneered by German sociologist Max Weber (Lunenburg and Ornstein, 2004).With little variation, this model has dominated educational system structure throughout the past century.

In the late 20th century, management theory began to focus more on collaboration and flat organizations and less on hierarchical methods of organization. The education field, which acknowledged the challenges and failures of bureaucratic structures, gradually began to adopt the language of this movement toward building "learning organizations" (Senge et al., 2000). While educational leaders speak the language and promote more collaborative cultures in their learning organizations, the primary means of organization remains rooted in a hierarchical structure where decisions are made at the top and are handed down to the lower levels through mandates with very little input from the faculty and staff assigned to the campuses. The decision-making process is quite often very lengthy, requiring multiple stages of review, revision, and approval from several supervisors. In large districts, information and communications between and among departments and campuses is complicated if not nonexistent.

In the book *Here Comes Everybody* (2008), Clay Shirky explains the difficulties faced by traditional hierarchical organizations as they strive to achieve their core missions:

> Running an organization is difficult in and of itself, no matter what its goals. Every transaction it undertakes—every contract, every agreement, every meeting—requires it to expend some limited resource: time, attention, or money. Because of these transaction costs, some sources of value are too costly to take advantage of. As a result, no institution can put all its energies into pursuing its mission; it must expend considerable effort on maintaining discipline and structure, simply to keep itself viable. Self-preservation of the institution becomes job number one, while its stated goal is relegated to number two or lower, no matter what the mission statement says. (p. 29–30)

The key statement in the passage quoted is this: " . . . its stated goal is relegated to number two or lower, no matter what the mission statement says." What happens in our schools if our stated goal of improving student learning is relegated to number two status because the efforts to maintain discipline and structure pull our resources of time, attention, and money away from the focus on learning? Can you think of specific instances where other issues took precedence over a focus on learning on your campus?

Now look at your typical contemporary school district. Visit your local school district's website and check off the following steps. Note how long it takes and how many levels of web pages were needed to find information.

_____ Locate a list of district departments. How many are there?
_____ Locate curriculum documents.
_____ Locate information about athletic facilities.
_____ Find a staff directory.
_____ Locate the technology equipment standards.

_____ Locate the weekly lunch menu.
_____ Locate purchasing procedures.
_____ Locate up-to-date employee memos.
_____ View the current district calendar and make note of how many district-level meetings are listed. Are they listed?

Are any of the documents located behind password-protected portals? Why? How many of the sources are web pages and how many are .pdf files (Adobe) that require downloading before they can be viewed? Why?

Here is another exercise. Stop what you are doing right now and look around your office. How many three-ring binders do you see? How many bookshelves are taken up with those binders? When was the last time you opened one of those binders? How useful is this printed information if you never refer to it, and how much waste occurs from the excessive printing of documents that simply sit on office and classroom shelves after the training, in-service, or meeting has ended?

The point of these exercises is to build awareness of the complexity of a typical district's organization. This complexity mirrors what Shirky describes above, and it begs the question: How good are we at staying focused on our number one priority of "educating all students"? If you have spent even one semester in an educational leadership position, you have enough experience to know the demands placed upon everyone in the system, and the difficulty in focusing on the mission when faced with numerous meetings, action items, the barrage of emails, endless and often redundant paperwork requirements, and the always unpredictable "emergency." Indeed, our school leaders are forced to spend much more time focusing on discipline and structure rather than focusing on instruction and learning experiences.

Conscientious education leaders should ask themselves: Is there a better way to manage all this information and communication? There is—and we call it a "wiki."

2

What Is A Wiki?

You might be surprised to learn that wikis are older than the recent Web 2.0 technologies that are so prevalent across the Internet. Wikis have been around since the mid-1990s when the first wiki, the WikiWikiWeb, was developed by Ward Cunningham. Wikis were initially used only by technology teams in the development of software and hardware systems. The word "wiki" is the Hawaiian word for "fast," and as you become more familiar with how wikis work you will see why that term is so appropriate. Wikipedia, perhaps the best-known wiki, on Jan. 27, 2011, defined "wiki" as

> . . . a website that allows the creation and editing of any number of interlinked web pages via a web browser using a simplified markup language or a WYSIWYG text editor. Wikis are typically powered by wiki software and are often used to create collaborative works. Examples include community websites, corporate intranets, knowledge management systems, and note services. The software can also be used for personal note taking. (http://en.wikipedia.org/wiki/Wiki)

Essentially, a wiki is a website that can be edited by anyone or by anyone with appropriate privileges if the wiki is restricted to registered users. Most important, a wiki is a website that can be edited by anyone, without needing to know HTML (hypertext markup language) or some other scripting language. At the most basic level, editng a wiki is as easy as editing a document in a word processor or an email. While wikis are simple to use, they can include added functionality that give the users a robust set of collaborative features including embedded media such as videos, streaming video, slideshows, shared calendars, databases, and RSS (Really Simple Syndication) feeds, to name a few.

Public Wikis vs. Enterprise Wikis

Despite the common misperception (due to media coverage of Wikipedia) that wikis are open documents vulnerable to vandalism, wikis can be tightly secured with access restricted to employees and staff. At the same time, sections of wikis can be open to the public to allow collaboration between the school and home. In order to understand this difference, we need to distinguish between a *public wiki* such as Wikipedia, and an *enterprise wiki*, which companies worldwide are adopting within their organizations. Wikipedia is an example of the use of crowdsourcing (Howe, 2006) on a large and public scale, whereas enterprise wikis, which are usually restricted to employees or registered users only, typically tend to be a method for knowledge management, project management, collaboration, meeting management, and communication within an organization.

Whereas enterprise wikis also rely on the "wisdom of the crowd" to develop knowledge and products in a collaborative space, the biggest differences between public wikis and enterprise wikis are access, control, and number of participants. Enterprise wikis provide functionality that allows pieces of content to be grouped together in what is usually referred to as "spaces." The spaces can be set up according to department, school, team, or project, and access to each space can be limited to specific users. Typically, enterprise wikis are not open to the public, and access can be tightly controlled by wiki administrators. Additionally, users are registered and their contributions monitored. One enterprise wiki can contain open spaces and closed spaces with access open or limited to all those spaces based on the school or organization preferences. Security on the enterprise wiki can allow read and write access, read-only access, or no access. High-end enterprise wikis also allow integration with other systems such as school or district email. As we will see in later chapters, even the free wiki hosting services offer many of these features and provide very effective security for education-related wikis, thereby allowing schools and districts a free alternative for learning about and getting started with wiki use in the organization.

Wikis, Google Docs, and Blogs— What's the Difference?

A common question in wiki workshops and presentations is "How are wikis different from blogs or Google Docs?" For inexperienced users the distinction between these tools can be quite muddy, but this distinction becomes clearer with exposure to each medium. If a strategic plan's goal is to increase and improve communication and collaboration across an organization with the use of these tools, it is helpful to first understand the different functions and features of each and the ideal uses of each.

The general purpose of a wiki is to improve the ability of a team or staff to collaborate on a variety of projects electronically in a more efficient manner than by using email or face-to-face meetings alone. Specifically, Wikis are an excellent tool for mapping out plans, documenting work and processes, and archiving information for future reference. Wikis are not good tools to use for collaborative creation of highly formatted documents that will later be printed for reproduction, collaborative development of spreadsheets, or presentations. Additionally, while they do allow for collaborative feedback on projects, they are not ideal for soliciting input in the form of surveys. However, Google Docs can be used for all of the above and with the use of widgets, Google Docs can be embedded and integrated with wikis.

Google Docs is the free online suite of applications created by Google. This suite of applications includes a word processor (documents), spreadsheet, slideshow presentation application, and a tool for creating online forms that can be used for surveys, feedback, and voting. Some schools and districts are exploring the adoption of Google Apps, which includes all of the Google Docs applications plus a few others as a replacement for the traditional Microsoft Office suite of applications. In addition to being free for use, Google Docs also incorporates the very helpful wiki feature of archiving of version history. This means that when a document is edited, each version is saved and can be viewed later. The document can also be reverted back to any earlier version. Each version is date and time stamped and the registered user who made the edits is listed for each version. Rather than making a choice between using Google Docs or a wiki, we recommend using both in an integrated approach to communication and collaboration. With time, most users will begin to more fully understand when and where each tool is best used.

Blogs on the other hand are completely different communication tools. Blogs should be thought of more as online journals, but journals that allow for interactivity between the author and the readers. Many education bloggers refer to the act of blogging as having professional discussions in a public forum. Each blog entry can be published only by one author, but all blogs allow for access by more than one registered author. Readers of blogs can then comment on each blog entry, but they are unable to edit the original post. Uses for this in a professional situation might include follow-up with training sessions by posting follow-up questions or short reviews, a place for discussions on a group book study, weekly updates to the staff from the administration or leadership team, or as a personal professional reflection space for individual teachers. Blogs are very versatile as professional learning tools, and many

FIGURE 2.1 Basic Features of Wiki Tools

Function or Feature	Wiki	Google Docs	Blogs
Publishing content	Yes	Yes	By single author only
Group contributions & collaborative writing	Yes	Yes	By comments on posts only
Commenting	Yes	Yes	Yes
Sharing files	Yes	Yes	One-way only
Inserting images, audio, video	Yes	Yes	Yes
Widgets for additional interaction	Yes	Yes	Yes
User controls	Yes	Yes	Yes
Privacy features	Yes	Yes	Yes
Chronological order	No	No	Yes
Version history of user edits	Yes	Yes	No
Users can edit other's work	Yes	Yes	No
Easily accommodates large amount of information	Yes	Yes	No
RSS feeds of content	Yes	Yes	Yes
Intended for development of content	Yes	Yes	No
Intended for publishing content	No	No	Yes

educators around the world have found the use of blogs very beneficial to their professional growth as well as to the growth of their students.

Figure 2.1 Basic Features of Wiki Tools summarizes some of the basic features of each of the tools described.

How these tools and others can support and extend wiki use is discussed in Chapter 7. A school or district that is planning to adopt the use of wikis should also consider adopting these other tools as a more comprehensive communication and collaboration strategy.

3
Why Use A Wiki?

A few of the many companies that are embracing wiki use in their organizations include Boeing, Best Buy/Geek Squad, BMW, Xerox, IBM, Disney, DHL, Procter & Gamble, Thompson Learning, Ford Motor Company, and Texas Instruments. These and other companies are finding that for communication, collaboration, and knowledge management, the use of wikis positively impacts productivity, lowers production costs, increases creativity and innovation, and improves overall team collaboration. This becomes increasingly critical as companies expand globally with dispersed teams working in different time zones. In the book, *Wikinomics: How Mass Collaboration Changes Everything* (2006), authors Don Tapscott and Anthony Williams predict that "as a growing number of firms see the benefits of mass collaboration, this new way of organizing will eventually displace the traditional corporate structures as the company's primary engine of wealth creation" (p. 1–2).

A Paradigm Shift

As we shall see in examples throughout this book, the culture that emerges from the use of a wiki aligns with Rensis Likert's System 4 Organization (see Figure 3.1 on p. 10) where subordinate ideas are solicited and used by administrators, communication flows freely in all directions, decisions are decentralized and made throughout the organization at all levels, and goals are set by group participation (Likert, 1967). Of course, this also requires leadership grounded in Theory Y, which assumes that educators are professionals who accept and seek responsibility (McGregor, 1960). Wiki adoption will not thrive under heavily bureaucratic structures that rely on directives and control.

FIGURE 3.1 Comparison of System 1 and System 4 Organization

Organizational Characteristics	*System 1 Organization*	*System 4 Organization*
Leadership	Little confidence and trust between administrators and subordinates	Subordinate ideas are solicited and used by administrators
Motivation	Taps fear, status, and economic motives exclusively	Taps all major motives except fear
Communication	One-way, downward communication	Communication flows freely in all directions
Interaction-influence	Little upward influence; downward influence overestimated	Substantial influence upward, downward, and horizontally
Decision making	Centralized; decisions made at the top	Decentralized; decision made throughout the organization
Goal setting	Established by top-level administrators and communicated downward	Established by group participation
Control	Close over-the-shoulder supervision	Emphasis on self-control
Performance goals	Low and passively sought by administrators; little commitment to developing human resources	High and actively sought by administrators; full commitment to developing human resources

Source: Likert, R. (1967). *The Human Organization*. New York: McGraw-Hill.

In his book *Wikipatterns: A Practical Guide to Improving Productivity And Collaboration in Your Organization* (2008), Stewart Mader explains why organizations across a variety of industries are beginning to use wikis:

> The wiki is rapidly growing in name recognition and use in organizations because its simple design and function enables equal

participation by people at all levels of technology knowledge and savvy. On top of that, it has an unprecedented ability to adapt to different uses, bring people together and strengthen teams, and promote a collaborative approach to problems. (p. 4)

The value for educational organizations, districts, and schools is that wiki technology is appropriate for novice users, which allows for an easy-to-use collaborative environment that can increase knowledge and cooperation across the entire organization. Additionally, because the wiki can be edited by anyone, it enables the "flattening" of the organization where everyone can contribute to the collective knowledge base as well as the planning and implementation of new initiatives, thereby generating more ownership of the initiatives. By bringing the organization closer to Level 4 Organization (Figure 3.1) than current models, the wiki creates a "paradigm shift" in terms of organization and participation. This shift is crucial to education organizations that have been striving to become "learning organizations" (Senge et al., 2000), but have yet to move away from hierarchical bureaucratic structures.

In addition to the organizational growth that is enabled by the use of wikis, electronic storage and email management are relieved by the reduction in "attachments" emailed across the organization. This will make email servers as well as employees much happier! The information and communication flow is clearly expressed in Figure 3.2 (page 12).

The European investment bank Dresdner Kleinwort Wasserstein is one example of the impact of wiki use on organization resources. Wiki use, which originated through an informal, grassroots process in their IT department, has now spread across the company and has resulted in a 75 percent drop in email volume and a 50 percent cut in meeting time, which in turn has resulted in greater productivity and more effective collaboration throughout the organization (Tapscott and Williams, 2007). Imagine that kind of reduction in email volume and meeting time in your school or district offices. How many more productive hours could your staff find in their current weekly schedules? How much of this time could they use to focus on instruction and student learning?

Let's explore a few examples of how your organization can be changed through the adoption of wikis.

Scenario: Principal Jones wants to see what other campuses are doing for student intervention

Before Wiki (B.W.)

He emails a few other principals who are friends of his on Monday morning. By that afternoon one of the other principals emails him back with a

FIGURE 3.2

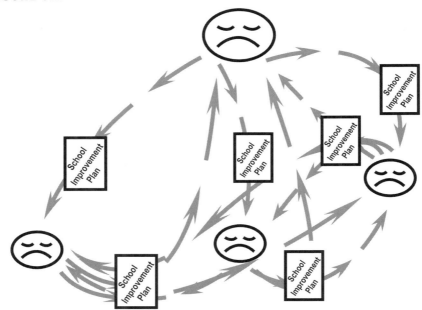

Email Collaboration

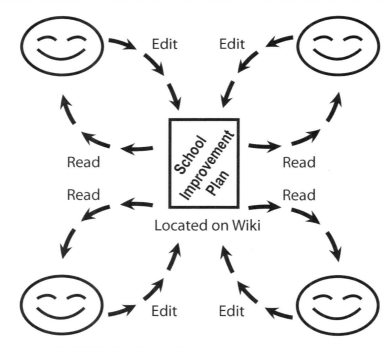

Wiki Collaboration

FIGURE 3.3

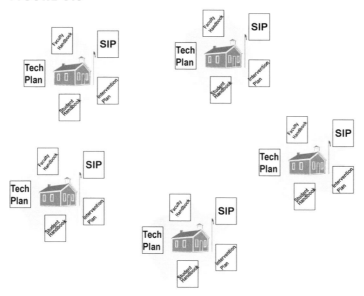

Word document. The next day two other principals email him back with brief explanations in the emails and another principal forwards the request to his dean of instruction to fulfill. By the end of the week he still hasn't heard from one of the principals. Figure 3.3 provides an example of how documents are scattered around the various campuses and are not easily accessible to personnel on other campuses.

After Wiki (A.W.)

Principal Jones searches on the word "interventions" in the district-wide wiki and within seconds has a list of all the intervention plans for every school in the district. The intervention plans, which are contained on their own pages within the wiki, are complete and up-to-date and provide him with a complete picture of what is happening on other campuses in his district. Figure 3.4 (page 14) provides an example of how documents and plans can be centrally located within a districtwide wiki. After Wiki (A.W.), all documents are located centrally on the wiki and are easily accessible to personnel on separate campuses.

Scenario: A team from Central High School attends a national education conference—paid for with school funds—with the expectation that they will bring back what they learn to the campus to share with other teachers.

14 ◆ Wikis for School Leaders

FIGURE 3.4

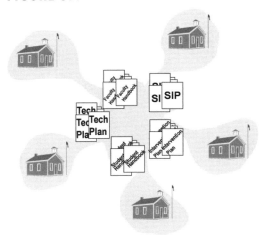

Before Wiki (B.W.)

Individual members of the team take notes in a variety of ways: one uses a laptop, two others use a notebook or a journal, and the last two just take notes on the back of handouts that they get at each session they attend. The team gets together on the last night at the conference to compare notes and discuss ideas for professional development sessions they can facilitate when they get back. Two months later they meet again to plan the professional development—some of the team members bring their notes to the meeting and some forget to bring their notes.

After Wiki (A.W.)

The team creates a conference wiki where each of them takes their notes while sitting in individual sessions. One page of the wiki is set up to build the professional development agenda that they will use when they return to campus. They list professional development session proposals on the page so the team can vote on the most relevant sessions to offer when they return. They meet briefly upon their return to campus to discuss logistics; then they share the complete agenda with the principal for approval. Two months later they deliver the professional development and share the entire wiki (including all their notes) with the entire faculty. (A more detailed description of this is highlighted in Chapter 4.)

Scenario: The district's director of curriculum wants to create an ad hoc committee to develop a curriculum for "digital citizenship and 21st century literacy."

Before Wiki (B.W.)

The director posts an announcement on the districtwide intranet; then he spends the next two months interviewing interested candidates as they stumble upon the announcement and submit their letters of interest. After two months the committee is seated, and they spend the next four months meeting once every two weeks for two hours after school. They eventually provide the director with a proposed curriculum presented in a three-ring binder.

After Wiki (A.W.)

The director performs a search in the wiki on the terms "digital citizenship" and "21st century literacy." The results include links to staff profiles and portfolios that include those phrases. The director sifts through the profiles to locate staff members who have been involved in related projects, then reviews their wiki activity to see who is most active in collaborating on a variety of projects. From the list, the director invites a selected group of staff members to interview for the committee. The interviews take less than two days. The committee members meet in person once every two weeks for two hours after school while also collaborating on a regular basis through the wiki. After one month they contact the director and ask her to review the proposed curriculum that they have developed on the wiki. The director approves the curriculum, and the wiki pages of the proposed curriculum are moved to the district's online curriculum wiki.

Scenario: A committee from Central Middle School needs to develop a five-day professional development schedule for August when the teachers return from summer break.

Before Wiki (B.W.)

The committee members spend the first few weeks emailing resources to each other with ideas for various kinds of professional development they can include during that August week. They schedule a meeting, but a couple of the committee members can't attend the meeting because of family commitments. The members who can meet come together without an agenda to just brainstorm and discuss some of the ideas that were emailed. The meeting ends with no firm decisions, and the team decides to meet again the following week. At the next meeting they are able to decide on some of the ideas, and they begin plugging ideas into the five-day schedule. They have three more meetings over the next month to finalize the schedule. A couple of the suggested sessions require contracts with external service providers and two committee members communicate with the service providers to arrange the dates and times of their sessions. Plans are still not finished by the end of the school year, and the committee has to meet two more times during the summer to complete the plans.

After Wiki (A.W.)

The committee has an initial organizing meeting to discuss a plan of action using the wiki. They create a wiki page just for planning and spend the next two weeks contributing ideas, voting on ideas, and plugging ideas into the wiki. After three weeks they meet again to review the current plan; then one of them emails the principal asking her to review the plan as it is on the wiki for approval. After the principal suggests a few revisions on the discussion section of the planning page, a couple of committee members make the suggested changes. Once the principal approves the plan, the committee uses the wiki to develop agendas, handouts, and presentations for the sessions that they have each volunteered to facilitate. Wiki pages are shared with a couple of external service providers who have been contracted to come in to provide professional development on some specific topics. By the end of the school year, the committee has created a good schedule for professional development. During the summer, the committee easily adjusts the plans as needed through the wiki with no need for any face-to-face meetings.

Scenario: The data team from Central Middle School needs to create a data inventory to have a summary of all internal and external assessments used in the school.

Before Wiki (B.W.)

The data team creates a table in a Word document, then emails it out to the entire faculty for input. By the end of one week the team has received replies from only eight staff members. One member of the data team takes all the replies that contain edited versions of the Word document and spends time copying and pasting all the edits from the individual documents into one document. The team sends out the document again to get more responses. After three weeks the team shares the entire inventory with the leadership team at their monthly meeting and finds out from some members of the leadership team that some assessments are missing from the inventory.

After Wiki (A.W.)

The data team creates a table on one page of the campus wiki and sends an email to the entire faculty with a link to the wiki page. They give the faculty a deadline of two weeks to input information they have on the various assessments used on campus. The data team emails the leadership team with a link to the wiki page so that the leadership team can monitor the development of the inventory, then discuss the results at their next meeting. At the next leadership team meeting, one member of the data team opens the wiki page on a laptop and fills in any missing information to complete the inventory at that time.

Scenario: The Central High School Senior Prom Committee wants input from the senior class on the theme, location, and menu for their upcoming prom.

Before Wiki (B.W.)

The committee holds a series of "town hall meetings" with the senior class to discuss options and to seek input. They issue a printed survey to the entire class at one of the meetings and later review the results at a second meeting. Results have to be tallied by hand.

After Wiki (A.W.)

The committee uses a wiki to share all of their planning information with the entire class. Locations are listed on the wiki along with hyperlinks that allow the class members to see the websites of the potential locations before voting. The committee embeds a survey using Google Forms into the wiki and sets a deadline for the class to review all options before submitting their choices through the online survey. The results are published instantly by embedding the Google Spreadsheet into the wiki page. All planning information and survey results are accessible to the entire school community including all students, teachers, administrators, and parents.

The Wiki Future Is Now

As you can see from these examples, there are many situations where wikis can be used to improve processes as well as individual and team productivity. With the exceptions of confidential student and employee information, most information within any school or district can be shared more effectively and more efficiently through the systemic use of an enterprise wiki. As with any change in practice, implementation of an enterprise wiki is not without challenges, and it will require persistence on the part of leaders. However, as with any effective change process, the most effective approach incorporates both a top-down and a bottom-up, grassroots, implementation. District or school leaders should set the groundwork by supporting the implementation and making the necessary changes within the system to ensure adoption across the organization. Locating and enlisting the assistance of "early adopters" at lower levels of the organization can be quite effective in spreading adoption through viral, grassroots methods.

In addition to the productivity benefits for the adults, the use of a wiki increases adult competency with this same technology that students will be using in the workplace as they complete their education. In fact, we are already seeing the use of wiki-like features in new web tools being developed every day. For example, Google Wave is a new tool that merges traditional email functionality with wiki functionality. Conversations in Google Wave can be edited by anyone who has subscribed to the Wave. This means that any information in a Wave can be corrected, appended, or commented on by any of the subscribers to the shared Wave. Another tool, Google Docs, includes the Docs word processor, spreadsheets, and presentations, and allows users (of shared documents) to edit all of the content and their edits are archived in a history that allows users to revert to previous versions. Wiki features such as these are increasingly being incorporated into nonwiki tools, and it is reasonable to expect that these functions will continue to spread across more and more applications.

Learning and using these tools in our own work allows us to understand and own the technology, which enables us to be more effective in helping students learn how to use these tools productively. These are the "workplace skills" that we need to be teaching, and we need to know how to use them in our own work as well. The U.S. Department of Education considers these skills so important that they address educator competency with these tools in the new National Education Technology Plan 2010. The full text of the plan can be viewed at http://www.ed.gov/technology/netp-2010.

The plan recommends that teachers model "connected teaching" where "teams of connected educators replace solo practitioners" and where connection replaces isolation.

> Classroom educators are fully connected to learning data and tools for using data; to content, resources, and systems that empower them to create, manage, and assess engaging and relevant learning experiences; and directly to their students in support of learning both inside and outside school. These same connections give them access to resources and expertise that improve their own instructional practices and guide them in becoming facilitators and collaborators in their students' increasingly self-directed learning. (p. xii)

Additionally, Will Richardson, an edublogger and author of *Blogs, Wikis, Podcasts and Other Powerful Web Tools for Classrooms, Edition 3* (2010), states that teachers have to be "colearners" who model their own use of these tools and must understand "the practical pedagogical implications of these technologies" in order to be effective in preparing students for a highly networked and global future (Richardson, *Educational Leadership*, 2008).

In the event of a natural or man-made disaster, another benefit to establishing the use of wikis in your organization is that a wiki provides an excellent medium for distance collaboration. If school and work are disrupted, for example, by extensive flooding, employees and/or students and teachers can stay in contact with one another and can continue working on critical projects regardless of whether or not schools or offices are closed. At any given time, there are schools that are coping with any number of natural disasters such as floods, hurricanes, blizzards, and earthquakes or other disruptions such as widespread illnesses and flu outbreaks. Some communities also cope with occasional man-made situations such as chemical or gas leaks at refineries, disruptions in the water supply, and fires. All of these situations have traditionally halted work and learning, but the use of a wiki can provide some remedy to the situation and allow at least some continuity of learning and work.

In Chapter 5, How?: Making It Work in Your Organization, we will explore the nuts and bolts of implementing the adoption of wiki use across your organization. First, Chapter 4, When & Where?, will explore some more specific examples of how wikis can be used across our schools and our districts.

Reflection Questions

How does the information in this chapter change your thinking around the use of technology in professional activities?

_____

_____

_____

What questions does this information raise for you?

_____

_____

_____

How might this information influence your work as an educator?

_____

_____

_____

4
When & Where?

As we have seen, the versatility of a wiki allows for a variety of uses within an education organization. Wikis can be useful for district office departments, intradistrict teams, school administration and leadership teams, campus department or grade level teams, and in a variety of other settings. In fact, wiki use can be unlimited with regard to nonsensitive information; however, no one should store student or employee personal information on a wiki. Even with that limitation, the impact of wiki use in a school or district office can dramatically improve nearly all operational processes.

Wikis for Leadership and Administration

School leadership is complex and demanding. Very few school administrators are successful in their leadership without good organization skills, effective time management strategies, and effective communication skills. Even with these skills, many school administrators struggle with competing demands for their time, crisis management, and an always overflowing in-box. The skilled and effective implementation of wiki use by a campus leader can be critical for anyone seeking a way to work smarter and not harder. As we shall learn, wikis provide educational leaders with an easy-to-use tool for archiving work, managing documentation and information, and more effective and efficient team collaboration.

Figure 4.1 (page 22) aligns educational processes and practices with corporate practices that are frequently managed or facilitated through the use of a wiki. While many of the uses listed in Figure 4.1 relate to collaborative team planning and documentation, wikis can also be used by individuals as a personal online "notebook" where information can be documented, organized, and archived. Resources can be uploaded or linked to within the wiki, and all

FIGURE 4.1

Business	Schools and districts
Collaborative intelligence	Professional learning communities
Documentation	Memos, policies and procedures, forms, and other documents
Participatory collective knowledge base	Professional learning communities Critical friends groups
Project management	Grant writing and grant program management
Tacit knowledge	Collection of veteran teachers' knowledge about instruction, classroom management, and pedagogy
Meeting management	Meeting agenda development Meeting minutes/notes Meeting archives
Encyclopedia	Curriculum and instruction clearing house/knowledge base
Business social networks	Professional learning networks, personal learning networks
Flexible client collaboration	School/home collaboration Collaboration with business partners

content can be easily transferred to other documents or other wikis depending on the need. This is one of the best ways to explore and learn about the use of wiki as it provides a private space for experimentation.

Communication and Knowledge Management

In *Change Leadership*, Tony Wagner outlines Seven Disciplines for Strengthening Instruction, and one of these disciplines is "Meetings About the Work." In his explanation, he criticizes the typical staff meetings that are concerned only with announcements and operations rather than the work of effective instruction. He explains that the usual agenda items would be better left to memos (and by implication—emails) in order to leave the meeting time for professional development around effective instruction or reflection on current instructional practices (Wagner et al., 2006).

Douglas Reeves also addresses what he refers to as "pointless meetings" in his book *The Learning Leader* (2006):

> Appreciation, recognition, and personal contact are some of the most extraordinarily strategic uses of leadership time, yet time is rarely allocated in that way because we are too busy with expenditures of time that are distinguished only by tradition and expectation, not by effectiveness. (p. 169)

By this he means that too often we insist on holding the typical monthly staff meetings or weekly team meetings out of habit, and that these habits result in wasted time. Both Reeves and Wagner suggest that we rethink how we spend our face-to-face time and that we save the announcements and "information sharing" for written memos.

A school or district could use a wiki for sharing announcements and operational information with staff members rather than using memos in .pdf format (Adobe), emails, or printed memos as Wagner specifically suggests. This would reduce paperwork and save precious storage memory in email accounts and on employee hard drives because the wiki is stored on a server, multiple copies are unnecessary, and all changes are archived on a server. Additionally, the wiki also allows leaders to plan and facilitate team meetings more effectively and efficiently from the planning stage through the follow-up stage. The stress of trying to coordinate with everyone's personal schedules is eliminated when participants have access to all documentation at all times from all locations, and when face-to-face interaction is not necessary. Participants are freed to collaborate at their individual availability.

In the 2008–2009 school year, the Curriculum, Instruction, and Assessment Division in the Houston Independent School District (Houston, Texas) began using wikis for collaboration among some of the division's curriculum teams. The first team to implement the use of wiki was the Adolescent Literacy Team. Initiated by the two members of the team, the wiki is

FIGURE 4.2

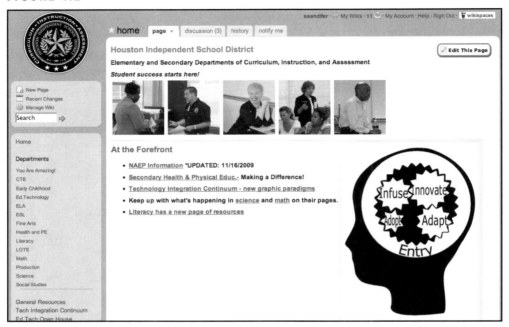

being successfully implemented within the entire Literacy Support Network, which spans all the middle schools and high schools within the district. The various uses include meeting agendas, notes, and feedback; storage of literacy related materials; hosting of slideshows, videos, and other professional learning materials; embedded feedback forms; hosting of photos and other artifacts of the collaborative work; pages for collaborative development of resources and documents (the team also uses Google Docs for collaborative writing and development of agendas, presentations, and documents); and a variety of other resources that contribute to the wiki becoming a "live" and collaboratively developed "Literacy Coach Handbook."

Users of the Literacy Support Network wiki include a variety of users at all technological skill and comfort levels. Despite this variation in skill levels, the overall consensus among the diverse group is that the wiki has become an essential component of the network's communication and collaboration activities. Technology-savvy users appreciate the ability to contribute their own ideas and knowledge to the wiki content, while less experienced users appreciate having all of the resources and content in one continually updated location. All members of the network know that they can find the answers to nearly all of their questions within the wiki, and many have adopted the use of wikis on their campuses to promote similar methods of communication and collaboration.

The Literacy Support Network wiki has become a model for other teams. During the 2008 fall semester, the English Language Arts Team and the A2TeaMS (Academy of Accomplished Teaching in Math and Science) team started their own wikis to use with the campus-based teacher leaders with whom they each work. By midyear the Educational Technology Team introduced a divisionwide wiki for knowledge management across all the curriculum teams within the division. The division has become "wikified" and many team members are beginning to understand the benefits provided by the use of wikis for all of the division's work. Two years later, the work of the department has filtered out to the schools where individual campuses and campus-based instructional teams have created their own wikis for collaboration and communication

The Houston Independent School District's Elementary and Secondary Departments of Curriculum, Instruction, and Assessment have developed a wiki for interdepartmental knowledge management and resource sharing. Launched in the fall of 2008, the new wiki is not only a space for collaboration and communication, it is also a place for the team members to learn and model 21st century skills. See Figure 4.2.

The Literacy Support Network's wiki provides a one-stop "shop" for all of the materials and resources required by the members of the network. A separate blog is also incorporated by embedding the blog's RSS feed. See Figure 4.3 on page 26.

Building Action Plans

Wikis can be used to build and maintain action plans including, but not limited, to school improvement plans, technology plans, grant proposals, departmental action plans, and special project plans.

Perhaps the most valuable of these is the use of a wiki for developing and maintaining a school improvement plan. In fact, a wiki as the school improvement plan could be the most collaborative, truly "living" document that drives school improvement on a daily basis. Rather than just working from multiple copies of an electronic text document (at best), the framework for the school improvement plan could be copied into a wiki and team members could make their edits directly into the wiki. This is one of those uses that works very well for freeing up email memory space. School improvement plan documents can grow to become quite large and if trying to collaborate via email with several team members they can quickly clog up multiple email inboxes as one copy becomes many copies across the team. Because considerations would have to be made with regard to structure, it might be helpful to

FIGURE 4.3

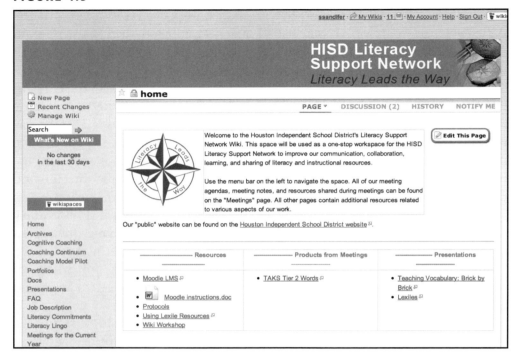

also make use of Google Docs for the initial drafting of the school improvement plan.

If you have ever worked on a grant proposal you are aware of the complexity of the task. The best proposals are usually drafted by a school team, and once again, as we have seen in the previous examples, a wiki (with or without the addition of Google Docs) is an excellent way to manage the collaborative writing process. Each section of the grant proposal can have its own wiki page and specific references of the research supporting the proposal can easily be linked to the original sources if they are online. If a district has a districtwide wiki, the grant management department could create wiki templates for the grant proposals and give each school its own space in which to draft their proposal, streamlining the process from beginning to end and making the process faster and easier for everyone.

Transform Meetings

One of the most powerful uses for a wiki across a school or district is the ability to transform the nature, structure, and function of all meetings. As we know, meetings can be one of the biggest drains on our scarce resource of time. How meetings are planned, structured, and facilitated can make a huge difference in productivity and outcomes within every education organization. A wiki can provide a means of improving many of the processes around meeting development, structure, and facilitation. Of course, a wiki is not a solution for poor facilitation, but those skills can be learned elsewhere and will be greatly enhanced by the use of a wiki.

How can transform meeting agenda development? Traditionally the meeting organizer sets the agenda for a meeting. At best, skilled facilitators who conscientiously plan productive meetings that add value for all participants create these agendas. At worst, these agendas are simply laundry lists of information items that are better communicated via email or memo. In the very best scenarios the skilled facilitator generates a skeleton agenda and shares it with participants in advance of the meeting to solicit additional items. A wiki can be an ideal place for collaborative meeting agenda development. All participants and stakeholders can access the wiki page and add their own agenda items prior to the meeting. The facilitator can review the proposed agenda items and rearrange the order, time, and resources needed.

The wiki becomes especially helpful when preparing for weekly status update meetings that are common among leadership teams. Usually these meetings take the form of a round-robin with the head administrator or a designated meeting facilitator asking each person, one at a time, to describe what they have done in the past week and what their plans are for the upcoming week. Too often these meetings are lengthy with information being discussed that does not apply to all meeting attendees. For those attendees the meeting takes time away from other work that they could be doing. Imagine instead that all status updates, progress, and weekly goals are added to a dedicated meeting page within a wiki. When the team comes together for the meeting, the question asked around the table changes from "What have you accomplished and what are your plans for the coming week?" to "Based on what you have written in the wiki, what resources do you need and what key points do the other members of this team need to be aware of with regard to your projects?" The result is a shorter meeting with more information shared among the team than in nonwiki-supported meetings. All detailed status updates are available on the wiki for review by any team member.

During any meeting, notes can be taken directly in the wiki. Depending on the nature of the meeting, one scribe can be selected to generate the notes on the same page as the agenda, or each participant can take his or her own notes on separate wiki pages that are linked from the agenda page. Either of these solutions are acceptable and a marked improvement upon the older scenario where one person takes notes on paper and later transcribes those notes to an electronic document, which is then emailed out to the participants. Can you see

FIGURE 4.4

the conservation of time that occurs when wikis are used for meeting notes? Depending on the nature and structure of the meeting, this method can save anywhere from thirty minutes for shorter meetings to a few hours for lengthier, more intensive meetings that require debate, brainstorming, and knowledge development. In the Houston Independent School District, meeting participants who have experienced this significant improvement in turnaround time for meeting notes have expressed a deep appreciation for this feature of wiki use.

So what happens after the meeting? In most cases, with the use of a wiki there is little or nothing that is required of the facilitator after the meeting. All participants have access to the wiki and all meeting documentation has already been added to the wiki either before or during the meeting. In some cases the facilitator may want to get feedback from the participants, which can be accomplished by creating a feedback form in Google Docs and embedding the form into the meeting wiki page. In other cases some of the meeting information may need to be crossed-referenced with other information located elsewhere in the larger wiki, and this is easily accomplished by creating hyperlinks to those items.

The Literacy Support Network uses its wiki for everything described on the previous pages. You can see in Figure 4.4 how a "meetings page is structured and in Figure 4.5 you can see what one of the meeting pages looks like after a meeting. Notice that the page for the meeting includes the facilitator's

FIGURE 4.5

agenda, an embedded slideshow, an embedded form for reflections, and the meeting notes.

Personal Portfolios

Some businesses have found it useful to allow employees to create "personal profiles" as separate wiki pages. When employees edit articles, their edits are tracked and linked back to the employees' personal profiles. This could be very useful in education organizations for several purposes. First, from a supervisory perspective, employee contributions to organizational knowledge can be easily tracked by viewing an employee's editing history on the wiki. This would be helpful for annual professional evaluations and when administrators are making decisions about assignments to leadership positions.

A second use of these personal profiles would be related to a decision-making process around the development of specific teams. For example, if an administrator wanted to create an ad hoc committee to research and make recommendations about a proposed initiative, the administrator could perform a search on the wiki for key terms related to the initiative. Employee personal profiles that have been set up to also serve as professional portfolios for each employee contain those key terms. From these search results, the administrator can generate a list of employees who have worked on similar committees or projects and who may have an interest in the proposed initiative. In other words, employee personal profiles and professional portfolios would allow administrators to track staff expertise, skills, and professional interests quickly and easily.

A third use is more social. Open personal profiles or professional portfolios would be accessible to all staff as well as administration. Staff members could perform searches for their particular areas of interest and through these search results they can locate other staff members who share similar interests. This would allow employees to network more easily with like-minded peers thereby increasing collegiality by nurturing a collaborative culture in which faculty and staff feel connected to more of their colleagues. While this may not seem like a priority to administrators and faculty who belong to the Baby Boom cohort, it is a priority for members of the Generation Y cohort and for many members of the Generation X cohort who are accustomed to social networking through online tools such as Facebook.com, MySpace.com, and LinkedIn.com. Members of Generation Y and many members of Generation X are inherently collaborative and networked due to their experiences with interactive online social tools. Veteran educators and educational leaders should not dismiss these social uses of technology as unimportant to employee motivation and job satisfaction as these will become increasingly more important as more members of Generation Y enter the profession (see A Closer Look: Generational Dynamics section that follows).

Creation of a personal profile or professional portfolio would be an excellent activity during an introductory professional development session on the use of an organization's enterprise wiki. You may find it helpful to provide faculty and staff with some minimal guidelines on what to include on their personal profile or professional portfolio page, such as

- Name and contact information
- Current position, campus/department, and professional interests
- Brief resume/CV
- Current projects or teaching assignments
- Links to personal websites (such as online professional portfolios
- LinkedIn.com profiles, professional blogs)

Wikis for Professional Learning and Faculty Collaboration

Professional Learning Communities

In *Professional Learning Communities at Work* (1998), Rick Dufour and Robert Eaker state that "educators seeking to create more effective schools must transform them into professional learning communities." Dufour and Eaker define Professional Learning Communities (PLCs) as teams that are focused on three priorities: learning, collaborative culture, and results. While PLCs do allow for a collaborative focus on learning and results, Dufour and Eaker warn that "the devil is in the details" in that educators are often given ambiguous, often conflicting advice on how to go about implementing PLCs on their campuses (DuFour and Eaker, 1998, p. 15). Not only is the concept often ambiguous to many educators—especially when the logistics of implementation are equally ambiguous to administrators—but the daily practice of operating in PLCs is fraught with issues around effective meeting facilitation and the ever-increasing paper load that comes with developing "collaborative plans" and "collaborative common assessments." Too often, the knowledge and work of the PLCs remains isolated within the team "silos," never seeing the light of day. From an administrative perspective, monitoring the work of the PLCs can be demanding and frustrating due to accessibility of the PLC documentation. If ever there was a need for more effective "knowledge management" on our school campuses, it is now with the growing trend of PLC implementation across the country.

Wikis allow for a more productive collaborative culture focused on learning and results. PLCs can use wiki pages to create and monitor S.M.A.R.T. (Strategic, Measurable, Aligned, Results-oriented, Time-bound) goals and action plans, develop common lessons, cross-reference lessons with collaboratively developed curriculum documents, and develop and record meeting agendas, notes, and action items. The use of a wiki will not replace the valuable face-to-face interactions of regular PLC meetings, but it can help make those face-to-face meetings more productive and meaningful by allowing team members to immediately record decisions, plans, and meeting notes in addition to providing a perpetually accessible record of PLC work. Administrators will appreciate the ease of accessibility to the work of each PLC. While specific student information should not be included on any wiki pages, a significant portion of the work generated by the team can be shared and archived.

Although rare, another challenge to implementing PLCs is having teachers who have no other colleagues in their content area with whom to collaborate. The professional learning needs of these teachers can be addressed by a

---

A Closer Look: Generational Dynamics

Incentives and motivators for Generation X and Generation Y are different from those for the Boomers. According to authors William Strauss and Neil Howe, members of Generation X seek to build strong families and are reluctant to sacrifice that goal for the sake of their careers. Generation Xers differ from their parents (the Boomers) in their unwillingness to accept a corporate culture that demands excessive hours and energy from its employees, and they prefer work environments that are generally more flexible, more "networked," and less bureaucratic (Strauss & Howe, 1997).

Not much has been written in the media about this issue and its impact on our educational systems, but the media has published extensive coverage of the "Generation Gap" in the corporate workplace. Educational leaders need to be aware of the shift that is occurring in order to develop, nurture, and retain potential future leaders from both the Generation X and Generation Y cohorts.

Thanks to their early life experiences as latchkey children, children of divorce, and blended families, Generation X has a "reactive mindset" that values independence and eschews institutionalism. They are suspicious of traditional forms of authority and want no part of this system (Strauss & Howe, 1997). Generation X leaders are more likely to adopt "servant leadership" traits and to work closely with members of Generation Y to integrate appropriate technologies that transform their work, their workplace, and their organizations in ways that are more conducive to flatter, more democratic and collaborative environments. Yes, Generation X as a whole is more interested in their families than money, and they will collaborate with Generation Y to achieve a work environment that allows for the balance that both generations seek in their lives.

> Some readers may be thinking that this is just simple generational stereotyping. While it is true that some Generation Xers think and act more like Boomers and some Boomers behave and act more like Generation Xers or Yers, these personal and professional characteristics are generally true for the vast majority of each of these generational cohorts, and these characteristics do impact the modern workplace. We can look around us and see this in action without ever knowing the generational dynamics theory proposed by Strauss, Howe, and other researchers.
>
> School districts are concerned about the number of Boomer leaders who will be retiring within the next several years. Unless current systems and structures change dramatically, the potential up-and-coming leaders will "opt out" of the leadership roles as they are currently structured. Perhaps this will be good for education. Perhaps tomorrow's leaders will "drop out" only to go out and, in the Generation X entrepreneurial way, finally engage in that education "reinvention" that Tony Wagner proposes (Wagner et al., 2006). Many educators already believe that Generation Y (and the Homeland Generation) students will eventually reinvent education to suit their own needs (through the use of emerging technologies), and perhaps those students will find willing leaders in Generation X who will enthusiastically help them with that reinvention.
>
> Current educational leaders can harness the enthusiasm and energy of the Generation X and Generation Y cohorts by encouraging and facilitating the use of social networking and web-based tools such as wikis throughout the organization. A "new teacher wiki" might be a great supplement to more traditional induction methods, and school or districtwide policies can be placed on the wiki in draft form to encourage and invite input from all staff members before finalization of the plans or policies. Rather than fear the changes and the technology, all educational leaders—regardless of their generational cohort—must embrace and own the use of these new tools in all aspects of professional work.

wiki that provides a medium for "virtual PLCs" across a district or region for teachers of specialized subjects.

Critical Friends Groups

According to the National School Reform Faculty (NSRF), a Critical Friends Group (CFG) is defined as "a professional learning community consisting of approximately eight to twelve educators who come together voluntarily at least once a month for about two hours. Group members are committed to improving their practice through collaborative learning" (para. 1). Conceived of and developed originally by the Annenberg Institute for School Reform, CFGs emerged in the early 1990s and have since spread throughout the world as an effective professional learning experience for reflective education professionals. At the NSRF Annual Winter Meeting in January of 2009, the first-ever Moving CFGs Online preconference session was convened. As a result of the discussions and work conducted during this session, a group of experienced CFG coaches began embarking on a yearlong exploration of conducting CFG meetings online using a variety of Web 2.0 and electronic communication tools. A wiki will be one of the many ways that this group will collaborate on shared learning, and wikis in general are being explored for their use, not only for virtual teams but also for supplementing more traditional face-to-face CFG experiences.

The Houston Independent School District Literacy Support Network wiki is being used for everything from collecting resources and keeping meeting agendas and notes to embedding training modules and reflection forms. This network has also experimented successfully with the use of wikis during regular weekly meetings as a way to capture meeting notes and as a replacement for the traditional sticky note chart paper. Small groups of network members are able to "scribe" their collective work on separate wiki pages—using the wiki pages in place of chart paper (saving money and time) and making the small group work immediately accessible to the entire network.

Other Team Collaboration Ideas

The University of Southern California's (USC) Center for Scholarly Technology (CST) wrestled with implementation of blogs and wikis in the classroom across USC, and over the past few years they have examined their implementation practices to refine how and why wikis are being used across their campus. In the fall semester of 2005, the CST identified six general approaches for how wikis could be implemented around campus, and in addition to the classroom/student uses of wikis for student journaling, personal portfolios, and collaborative project knowledge bases, the CST also found the wikis useful for faculty practices such as research coordination and collaboration, curricular and cross-disciplinary coordination, and conference and colloquia website/coordination (Higdon, 2005). While these faculty uses are somewhat different from faculty practice at K–12 campuses, they do resemble others such as the PLC collaborative work described earlier in this chapter as well as district- level curriculum development practices and school or district activities and events.

A wiki can also be an effective place for a team to collaboratively share resources that some have direct access to but others do not. Members who belong to certain professional organizations may have access to online archives as a benefit of membership. Should a nonmember need to get an article for research purposes, he or she could access the material via listed team members who do have access to this material.

Lesson Plans

Wikis can be used as a method for storing and sharing lesson plans. In many schools, teachers are required to develop lesson plans and submit them to their supervising administrator. In a school that uses a wiki for communication and knowledge management, teachers can post lesson plans to a wiki space designated specifically for them. Administrators can easily pull up the wiki each week to see updated lesson plans. This would result in either a reduction of emails or a reduction in printed copies depending on how a school currently handles this requirement. This also meets the PLC principle of transparent professional practice while serving as an excellent way to capture the knowledge of veteran teachers.

The structure of a wiki used for lesson plans can vary according to the needs of the specific campus. Pages can be structured by date, by teacher, or by subject area, with teachers posting as needed in the appropriate page. Administrators or other teachers can easily locate weekly lessons by using the search function of the wiki to find lessons posted by specific teachers or from specific subject areas. Administrators who use RSS aggregators can easily subscribe to the RSS feed for that particular wiki in order to get weekly updates sent directly to their RSS aggregator.

Curriculum Mapping

As the wiki begins to "house" lesson plans, the school or district can implement the use of wiki for the purpose of some aspects of curriculum mapping. In their most basic form, curriculum maps allow faculty and administration to see how the entire scope and sequence of all curriculum areas relate to one another. Curriculum maps are helpful to interdisciplinary teams who are interested in aligning all curricula horizontally and vertically across multiple disciplines. Some schools and districts have started to invest in the purchase of software that allows for much more robust and comprehensive curriculum maps that also include assessment and measurement details in addition to curriculum and instruction information. However, for schools or smaller

FIGURE 4.6

Grading Periods (right) Subject Areas (below)	1	2	3	4	5	6
Algebra I	Patterns & Multiple Representations Proportional Reasoning	Algebraic Properties & Solving Linear Equations Proportional Reasoning & Algebraic Properties & Solving Linear Equations	Rate of Change & Intercepts Writing & Graphing Linear Equations Line of Best Fit Systems of Linear Equations	Systems of Equations & Inequalities Polynomials & Exponents Quadratic Functions pt. 1	Quadratic Functions pt. 2 Probability & Statistics	Exponential Functions & Inverse Variations Bridge to Geometry
English I		Fiction Reading - Tragedy	The Media Coming of Age	Assessment Practice	Marxism, Totalitarianism, Communism Historical Fiction - Animal Farm	
IPC	Scientific Method, Measurement, and Safety Force & Motion	Machines & Efficiency Heat Electricity	Sound and Waves Light Energy Resources	Properties & Classifications of Matter Physical & Chemical Changes Atomic Structure	Bonding & Periodic Table Chemical Reactions	Solutions Acids & Bases Nuclear Energy
World Geography	Patterns in Our Physical World Patterns in Our Human world	US and Canada Mexico, Central America, and the Carribean	South America Europe	Russia and the CIS Africa	Southwest Asia South Asia	East & Southeast Asia The Land Down Under - Australia, New Zealand, Antarctica
Geometry						
English II						
Biology	Safety Nature of Science and	Molecules of Life: DNA to Protein	Organic Molecules Cells and Organelles	From Cell to System Human Body System	Evolution Taxonomy	Plant Kingdom Global Issues

districts that have not made such an investment, wikis offer a lower cost alternative to create very basic curriculum maps.

Each content area can create separate wiki pages for each major unit or in smaller units if the team chooses, and these units can be indexed on a central wiki page that contains a matrix that shows the order and content focus of all units. Each content focus title links back to the original page, but the matrix allows users to view all the curricula at a glance. This structure enables the curriculum team to identify gaps in sequencing order across the curriculum while also strengthening the development of professional learning communities that learn together through their collaborative work. For example, through the mapping process a team might notice that an eighth-grade science unit relies on students knowing certain math content before that particular math content is taught in the eighth-grade math area. The awareness of this misalignment provides an excellent opportunity for interdisciplinary collaboration, and ideally provides an outcome that results in a more coherent and better aligned curriculum across the board. Figure 4.6 shows how a matrix may be created on a wiki to help educators with very basic curriculum mapping. Each of the unit topics are linked to pages that provide more in-depth information while the matrix allows for a "big picture" view of the entire curriculum.

Professional Development

One challenge that schools and districts face is a shortage of time and money to send everyone to conferences and workshops. When faculty and staff members are able to attend, the challenge becomes how to facilitate the sharing of knowledge. Then, collecting and disseminating conference materials and knowledge by using a wiki is highly effective. A wiki can be set up so that each conference or workshop attendee can add articles as they attend sessions, take notes, collect knowledge, or highlight new ideas gathered in informal discussions and scouting the vendor floor. Sharing this information through the wiki provides solutions for leaders who want to ensure that funds expended benefit the whole organization.

Site-Based Professional Development

Site-based professional development can also benefit from the use of a wiki. Faculty and staff members who facilitate on-site professional development can use a wiki to plan the sessions and agendas, and they can either use sections of the wiki as the informational handouts or upload .pdf copies of handouts directly into the wiki for attendees to download to their own computers. To extend this idea even further, facilitators might allow attendees to create their own pages within the wiki for the purpose of taking notes during the sessions. By adding their pages to a page designated as a "directory," all notes are shared by all attendees, which allows for increased sharing of knowledge and insights. The notes along with the session agendas and handouts are all contained within one wiki and become part of the organizational knowledge "archive." A school team can use a wiki to organize their notes and resources gathered from attending a conference, thereby making it easy for all faculty to access the information for professional development. See Figure 4.7 on page 41.

For leaders who want better ways to document site-based professional development—especially for grant or funding purposes—what better way to do it than through a wiki? The wiki also becomes a professional development session "sign-in sheet" as the list of "recent changes" automatically provides an accurate accounting of all participants as they create and edit their own note pages.

A wiki can be used in place of a 3-ring binder for faculty resources. This wiki (see Figure 4.8 on page 41) was developed on one campus to replace the more traditional "Teacher Instructional Resources" manual that faculty usually received at the beginning of the year. All faculty members can edit the content to add specific examples of each instructional strategy from their

A Closer Look: Tag-Teaming Conferences

It is nearly impossible to send everyone to all national and regional conferences—there just is not enough time or money. Even if you have the money, there's no way you could get everyone off campus in the middle of the year, and many teachers choose to teach summer school (limiting their ability to take advantage of summer conferences). So what is an innovative and caring school administrator to do? How can you take advantage of these learning opportunities for your entire staff when time and money are scarce? As a campus administrator, I received those colorful and intriguing flyers describing upcoming conferences and workshops in my mailbox almost weekly, and I always wished I could send my entire staff to several of these each year. Unfortunately, I needed my teachers to be in the classroom with our students, and there was never enough money to send everyone anyway. So why even dream?

Dreaming provides an opportunity to find creative solutions to our problems. In this case, our campus was able to develop a solution that allowed us to take advantage of some of the conference offerings while also sharing new learning with the entire campus. Using a variety of funds (e.g., general funds, Title I, some grants), we made the decision to send a team to about three conferences per year—one each for summer, fall, and spring. The strategy includes three very important components:

1. Send a different team to each conference or institute (use a full faculty roster to keep track of this) and be sure to include a representative from each department as well as an administrator.

2. Team members must make a commitment to giving a presentation or setting up some kind of professional development for the whole staff within four months after returning from the conference.

3. Provide time or a schedule to support the on-campus training provided by the conference attendees.

The most effective strategy that we have found for No. 3 (providing time) has been to create a miniconference with a variety of concurrent sessions that the staff can choose to attend on a full professional development day. This takes some preplanning, which can easily be accomplished with the use of wiki. The results are well worth the efforts.

Large conferences usually provide a tentative conference planner online or in print before the opening day of the conference. By carefully using the conference planner to select strands or specific sessions, the team can plan their session before leaving campus. The team can complete the planning by using a table on a wiki page. If six people attend the conference, and those six people are able to sit through three to four sessions per day for three days, the total of sessions attended equals fifty-four to seventy-two different sessions. That is a lot of learning! If all the session notes are captured on a wiki, your team returns to the campus with a tremendous amount of new knowledge to share with the staff. All of that new knowledge is instantly available through the wiki. In fact, during the conference, nonattendees can access the wiki daily to see what new knowledge the team is gathering each day.

The emergence of blogging and other Web 2.0 tools increases the opportunities to share new learning with other faculty who are not able to attend the conferences. Perhaps you could have a "home team" of faculty members who attend the conference virtually. This home team could aggregate RSS feeds from conference bloggers to do any or all the following:

- collect information on a variety of sessions or specific strands
- collect information from presenter websites and wikis
- communicate information back to conference attendees (from their own campus)
- conduct additional research on specific topics of interest to the whole team and begin compiling resources for use when everyone is back on campus

This "home team" may consist of faculty who are interested but who are not able to attend for a variety of reasons—young children at home during the summer, teaching summer school, or vital core staff who cannot be out of the classroom during the school year. Two key components of this strategy include the Team Blog and the Team Wiki.

The Team Blog

Each team member can be an author, and he or she can use the blog to do live-blogging sessions, post photos, or just publish daily summaries of what was learned at the conference. "Home Team" members can subscribe to the blog and get daily updates from their colleagues who are at the conference.

The Team Wiki

Similar to the blog idea above, a team wiki could be set up so that each team member could add articles as he or she attends sessions or to

> highlight new ideas gathered in informal discussions and scouting the vendor floor. The wiki could also be a place to collect ideas for a "miniconference" that the team will organize when they return to campus, and the team could draft the miniconference agenda directly onto a page in the wiki. One page of the wiki could also be a place for the team to collect a "wish list" of stuff that they see on the vendor floor and want to learn more about for use on campus.
>
> You can combine both ideas above and link both through linked RSS feeds (blog includes RSS feed from wiki and wiki includes RSS feed from blog). As team members attend sessions, all their notes are collected in one (or two) places and the entire team has instant access to everyone else's notes. This saves time and increases the shared learning that can occur during attendance at such a large conference.
>
> Other tools to consider include Google Docs (and Spreadsheets and Presentations), websites Delicious.com and Diigo.com (for Social Bookmarking), and Twitter.

classroom which makes the entire resource much more dynamic than the more traditional binder, which could only be changed once per year.

Wikis for Home-to-School Communications and Collaboration

The National PTA recommends that schools and parents be "on the same page," share information, and form a communication team that consists of parents, teachers, students, and school administrators in order to improve home-school communication (National PTA, 2000, p. 31). A wiki can facilitate this process by allowing the communication team to collaborate on the development of home-school communication policies and practices.

A PTA/PTO wiki can incorporate a variety of components that include anything from pages used to collaboratively plan meeting agendas and school events to providing a space for the PTA/PTO and school to share current announcements and upcoming events. Calendars can be built into the wiki space to improve communication of upcoming events to the broader community.

The school can use the wiki space to publish information to parents including tips and advice on how they can support student learning at home and outside of the school day. Pages on the wiki space can also be dedicated

FIGURE 4.7

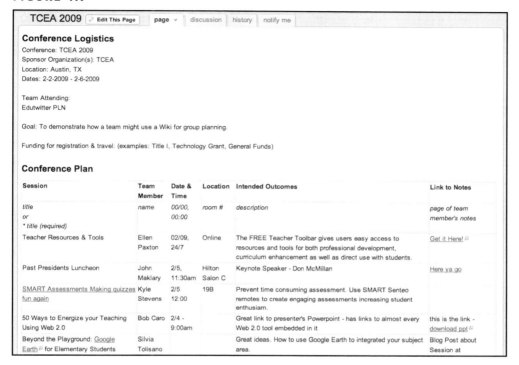

FIGURE 4.8

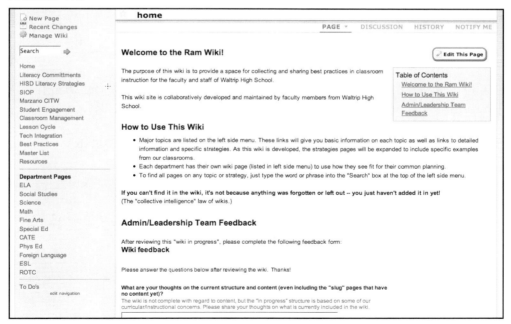

to planning volunteer activities on the campus, soliciting input from parents on school decision making, and providing contact information on faculty and staff to parents and the community.

If the school is in the process of improving or increasing its community business partnerships, the wiki would also be an excellent medium for providing information to prospective business partners on how they can support the school and the benefits that the school can provide to the partner.

School administrators can increase the use of the wiki by providing parents with access to computers during the school day. Some schools have created "Parent Centers" on their campus that are open during school hours to any parents who do not have Internet access at home. The parent center, which is usually located in a small room or office space, has Internet-connected computers (anywhere from five to fifteen) that parents can use for research, job searching, resume writing, and other personal business activities. The parent center can also be used to host events such as "Coffee with the Principal" and technology training sessions for parents and community members.

The Westlake High School PTO in Austin, Texas, has a PTO wiki (hosted on PBWorks) for communicating with the school community. The information contained within the Westlake PTO wiki includes recent news, contact information for PTO officers, volunteer opportunities, fund-raising activities, information on special PTO sponsored projects, and meeting minutes. On the home page of their wiki, the PTO states that one of its reasons for using electronic media is to communicate "greener."

> We have historically made copies of PTO minutes and meetings agendas available at our meetings, but these sets of paper copies waste resources and consume PTO funds to produce. Let's do better! Beginning this year, we will make minutes and agendas available via professional development, so you can read them, save them, review them online, and come to meetings just a little better prepared! (2009)

The Westlake PTO wiki includes basic membership information, details on fund-raisers, and documents used throughout the year. See Figure 4.9.

In summary, uses for PTA/PTO wikis may include the following (from http://wetpaint.com):

- Sharing mission statements, officer profiles, and contact info
- Keeping members up-to-date on what is happening with the organization
- Creating calendar pages to track all PTO events during the school year
- Compiling and sharing fund-raising plans, ideas, and event feedback

FIGURE 4.9

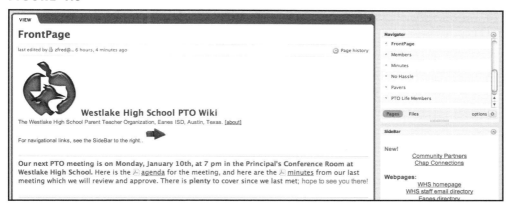

- Posting meeting agendas, notes, and tracking follow-up action items
- Creating volunteer sign-up pages for events, errands, etc.
- Posting picture galleries, slideshows, and clips of PTO events
- Sending messages via the wiki to share news, solicit information, or collect feedback
- Easily attaching copies of all standard forms (membership, volunteer forms, etc.)

Wikis in the Classroom

The concept of using wikis in classroom instruction has been covered extensively in a number of books, blogs, and websites. Educators around the world are discovering the value of wikis for engaging students in real-world collaborative learning with 21st century tools. A simple Google search for "wikis in education" brings up more than 19,000,000 results! Most arguments for the use of wikis in the classroom revolve around the issue of preparing students for global communication and collaboration, which will surely be a component of the 21st century workplace that they will enter upon leaving school. In this section we want to focus instead on the basic literacy skills that can be developed through appropriate use of wikis in the classroom as well as the advanced 21st century literacy skills that wikis require of users—skills that students will develop through the use of wikis in their learning experiences.

The U.S. National Institute for Literacy provides the following definition for literacy:

> The Workforce Investment Act of 1998 defines literacy as 'an individual's ability to read, write, speak in English, compute and solve

problems at levels of proficiency necessary to function on the job, in the family of the individual and in society.' This is a broader view of literacy than just an individual's ability to read, the more traditional concept of literacy. As information and technology have increasingly shaped our society, the skills we need to function successfully have gone beyond reading, and literacy has come to include the skills listed in the current definition (U.S. Department of Education, para. 1).

By the definition provided by the United States government, literacy is defined much more broadly than just reading and writing. The Houston Independent School District adopted a definition of literacy that includes "the ability to read, write, speak, listen and think effectively" (Houston Independent School District, 2008). Those terms encompass nearly anything we do when we interact with other people or with information whether it is in print, on the web, or incorporated in static visuals, video, or audio. In the past few years we have begun to hear terms such as "21st century literacy skills," implying that the skills that students need today are different from what they needed yesterday. Students today operate in a world very different from the one in which we adults grew up, but while the media that students engage with may be different, the media still require students to use skills that apply to all old and new media—the ability to read, decode, comprehend, write fluently and clearly, to articulate their thoughts orally as well as in writing, and to listen for understanding. These essential basic literacy skills have not changed. One can argue that hypertext (text that links to other text) transforms reading from a linear activity into a nonlinear activity, but in some ways reading nonlinear hypertext on the Internet is not so different from the "choose your path" fiction that we read as adolescents.

What is not debatable is the sad fact that adult literacy remains a serious problem in our society with recent studies indicating that 1 in 7 adults are functionally illiterate (Toppo, 2009). Without dramatic changes in the way we facilitate student learning, this statistic will not change. The fact is that in too many schools we are still using teaching methods that resulted in this high rate of illiteracy, and unfortunately we are using these methods today with students who are even less engaged with the curriculum than were previous generations. Even more daunting is how literacy needs have increased and the skills considered basic for employment, college, careers, and even the military have increased beyond what was considered basic for older generations. Technology has changed the way we work as well as the way we learn, regardless of the debate around the concept of 21st century literacy and skills.

As Judith Irvin (Irvin, Meltzer, & Dukes, 2007) explains in *Taking Action on Adolescent Literacy*,

Understanding the relationship between literacy and technology means that schools should examine: what types of academic literacy habits and skills are needed to prepare students for the future they face; how contexts for conducting research, learning, reading, and writing have changed because of the available technologies; and how assignments, teaching goals, and understandings about literacy have shifted. (p. 8)

As I was describing how a wiki works to one of my colleagues who specializes in adolescent literacy, she looked at me with astonishment as I explained the process of editing and revising and said "That in itself is an entirely new literacy!" She was referring to the aspect of wiki editing that allows users to review all edits made on the wiki and to be able to track participation as well as to revert to previous edits if needed. She realized that the ability to understand the structure and function of a wiki was something that would have to be explicitly taught to users before they could effectively use the wiki in a fluent manner.

If we consider the fact that wiki use in corporate America is becoming more widespread, then there are arguments for using wikis in the classroom in order to explicitly teach students "wiki literacy" in preparation for their future careers that will surely demand online collaboration. Additionally, if designed properly, projects that require the use of a wiki (by the students) will also help to build critical thinking skills as well as editing and revising skills. A wiki can be a powerful tool for helping students develop skills in critical analysis and review of information. They can "fact-check" the contributions of others and make immediate changes if necessary. For the teacher—as well as the students—the structure of the wiki allows for facilitator-monitored or self-monitored participation. As all changes are tracked by user, any user can easily see if all members of a group are participating equally in the creation of the knowledge.

Within the classroom, students can use wikis for a variety of purposes:

- Workspaces for individual or group projects
- Student-created textbooks
- Individual portfolios
- Interdisciplinary knowledge base
- Virtual projects with other schools or community partners

In addition to building adolescent literacy skills, teachers can also use wikis for more administrative tasks in and outside of the classroom. This accomplishes two goals: building teacher capacity in the use of new technologies and providing professional models of technology use for students. Teachers can use wikis for many purposes:

- Class notes and lesson summaries
- Parental and student communication
- Handouts
- Course syllabus
- Course links and resource notes
- School or class calendar
- Collaborative note-taking
- Concept introduction and exploratory projects
- Dissemination of important classroom learning beyond the classroom
- Teacher information page
- Student-authored books
- School newspaper

Student Voice and Leadership

Wikis provide an excellent medium for student voice and leadership. Not only does a wiki provide a place for documentation of the work of student clubs and organizations, it also allows that work to be more public and easily accessible to the entire school community. Some schools allow student leadership organizations and special interest clubs to create their own wikis while others create one wiki dedicated to all clubs and organizations. Allowing each to have their own wiki does provide the students with the ability to customize their own wikis, but having one centralized wiki may allow for more structure and focus that will be appreciated by faculty, administration, and parents. With one centralized wiki, each club and organization can have its own page or space with subpages added on for each of their individual projects. An example of this is shown in Figure 4.10. A few of the many uses of student wikis include:

- Student council meeting minutes, project planning, etc.
- Portfolio of student council work, documentation of procedures and processes
- Information related to schoolwide events like blood drives and donation campaigns
- Meeting minutes of grade level councils
- Prom planning, class voting on specific aspects of prom plans

FIGURE 4.10

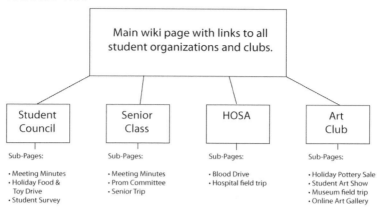

- Student research, surveys using Google Forms can be embedded in a wiki page with the results posted on another page
- Student newspaper/magazine (rather than on paper or in addition to paper)
- Yearbook documentation of production and input request from classmates
- Art exhibitions, art sales, field trips, and even an online art gallery right in the wiki
- All clubs and organizations' reminders about upcoming meetings, meeting topics, and other group events
- General information for all students on how to become more involved with the school's many clubs and organizations

One high school has even used a wiki to combat the use of websites such as RateYourTeacher.com. This example requires a great deal of trust between faculty and students and will require quite a bit of monitoring and moderating to avoid inappropriate language and statements. The school has set up a wiki where students write, moderate, and edit reviews on teacher classrooms. The reviews focus on classroom climate, instructional activities, and honest assessments—from the student's perspective—on how engaged all students are in the learning activities. Obviously, this also requires very specific agreements between the faculty and students on what can be discussed in the rubrics, and the reviews are moderated to ensure that each review is written in a constructive and positive way that encourages all stakeholders to make efforts to improve the overall learning environment of the school. Teachers are able to read the reviews and use these reviews, in addition to student grades and test scores, to make collaborative curriculum and instruction decisions with the goal of improving learning outcomes. Students use the reviews to develop a better understanding of the expectations and requirements of each class they are taking or plan to take. It goes without saying that this example is only possible in a school that has developed a strong collaborative culture with students and staff who are well experienced with using wikis and other technology in their learning and work.

Security Issues

Despite the common perception that wikis are open to the world for viewing and editing, all wikis allow information to be secured at the page or article level. This means that certain sections of the wiki can be open to the public, that is, parents and students, for the purpose of sharing curriculum and lesson plans while more sensitive information such as common assessment drafts can be secured and accessible only to relevant staff members. The public space of the wiki, especially that containing information such as curriculum and lesson plans, can be designated as "read only" to parents and students in order to prevent pranks and vandalism by students.

While wikis used for faculty and staff collaboration should be secure to prevent vandalism and spamming, wiki organizers should consider making as much of the wiki as public as possible to improve transparency in planning. This is especially true for sections of the wiki that include documents or information important to the broader school community, such as parents, local residents, business partners, and other community stakeholders. Remember always that the overall purpose of the wiki is to increase collaboration and not to just create another static website that can be edited only by one or two people.

Wikis used in the classroom should also be monitored and secured from vandalism or spamming from outside sources, but be careful about locking down the wiki so much that students miss out on the benefits of using a wiki to collaborate with others outside of their classroom and outside of their school. Collaboration with other schools, classrooms, or business/community partners should be structured to ensure a quality learning experience, but it is possible to do this very safely and successfully. A great example of how this can be done is the Flat Classroom Project (http://flatclassroomproject.net), which links classrooms around the world to each other and to industry experts in an effort to engage students in real-world collaborative learning on topics focused on digital citizenship and trends in information technology. In the Flat Classroom Projects, classes are linked by teachers, and their students collaborate on teams that consist of students from the different classrooms around the world. They use the wiki to develop their ideas and to post their finished work. Student identities are protected by using either coded usernames or by using a common method that includes first names and last initials only.

A general rule of thumb for all wikis that are used by students is to ensure that students do not use their full names for their user names. Most schools adopt a policy of using students' first names and last initials to avoid easy identification of individual students. In the classroom, teachers can use this method to still track student contributions to the wiki, but allow for some privacy and security.

The need for safety and security when using any technology is always important. However, the use of web tools is actually much safer than media reports would have us believe, and there is no reason to not explore the use of these tools because of safety/security concerns. There are ways to make wiki use safe, secure, and successful for everyone.

Reflection Questions

In what areas could you use a wiki in your school or district?

_____
_____
_____

What are the challenges you face for each of those purposes?

_____
_____
_____

What supports are currently in place that would make wiki adoption easier?

_____
_____
_____

5

How?—Making It Work in Your Organization

"The adoption and diffusion of an innovation within an institution does not guarantee its successful integration into the curriculum or its continued use."

—V.H. Carr Jr.

If you build it, they will collaborate, right? Not so fast. As with any new initiative, adoption and implementation will fail without an effective approach. A top-down mandate in and of itself will not be sufficient, especially considering the wide range of technology skill and comfort levels among staff members. A bottom-up grassroots effort will also fail without proper and appropriate administrative support. A balance between the two is needed for adoption of wiki use throughout an organization.

A careful analysis of how wikis have been successfully implemented on a variety of K–12 and college campuses reveals that the most successful implementations were those where the users were allowed to shape the structure of the wikis and make decisions on how to use the wikis to fulfill their own individual or team objectives. These successful implementations, while supported by administration, were not mandated in a top-down manner (Lamb, 2004). This is an important recommendation that bears repeating: Administrators and organization leaders must resist the urge to dictate or impose too much structure on the wiki as this can inhibit or stall adoption of the wiki by faculty and staff.

We can reflect on efforts to implement email use within education organizations over the past ten to fifteen years. In some cases, there are still pockets of practice today where information or items that could easily be emailed to colleagues are instead shared in print form, or worse, in lengthy "pointless"

FIGURE 5.1

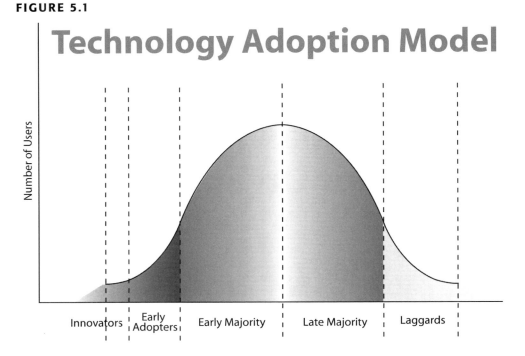

meetings. Email has still not successfully infiltrated all possible communication areas within our schools and districts, and researchers have found that some educators are slow to adopt email and other technologies due to a lack of effective training, a lack of access to easy-to-use applications or systems, increased acceleration of emerging technology trends, inadequate administrative support, the individual's lack of hands-on experience and/or the individual's general technology anxiety level (Shelley, 1998). Reflecting on this, no one should expect wiki adoption and implementation to happen overnight. Keep in mind Moore's Technology Adoption Model (Figure 5.1) and know that while "innovators" and "early adopters" will eagerly explore nearly any new technology to determine how and where it can enhance their work, it takes sustained effort and effective strategies to encourage the "early majority" to adopt technology. The "late majority" will usually adopt the technology after it has been in use within the organization for a period of time, but remember that some staff may never use the wiki (Moore, 1991.)

However, there are steps that schools and organizations can take to foster a climate more conducive to wiki adoption. In order to successfully implement wiki use, we must first understand "lessons learned" by other schools that have taken on the process of implementation and adoption of wikis.

Dos & Don'ts

Do provide access to the wiki outside of district or school intranets.
Adoption will happen more quickly if staff can access the wiki from any location and not just from the office or campus. Password protection can be used for sensitive information. The ultimate goal of using a wiki is to improve communication and collaboration in such a way that there is also an improvement in productivity. Limiting users to access only in the office defeats that purpose and will ultimately result in a failed attempt at wiki adoption. There is often a temptation to keep web-based applications secured behind the organization's intranet, but this should be avoided with a wiki. In order to promote adoption, it should be easily accessible and easy to use. Keep it simple.

Do encourage "grassroots" adoption.
If your entire organization or school is not yet ready to plunge into system-wide wiki use, allow smaller groups or teams to create their own wikis. These wikis can serve as models for future wikis and all the content can be easily transferred to a systemwide enterprise wiki when or if one is implemented. Be supportive of these grassroots efforts and highlight their accomplishments when appropriate so that the other staff members become aware of how the wiki use is contributing to the organization.

Don't impose an overly strict structure to the wiki. Do allow employees to define a structure that meets their needs as often as possible.
Start with a skeletal structure and allow employees the flexibility to change that structure as needed. The content that develops will ultimately dictate a certain structure but it is almost always nearly impossible to know exactly what that content will consist of and how it will need to be structured. Allow for an organic, flexible, and evolving structure from the beginning of wiki implementation.

Don't block access to free wiki sites such as Wikipedia, PBWorks, or WetPaint.
These free sites offer all staff members an easily accessible and easy-to-use space where they can explore how to use wikis by creating their own for personal use. A staff member may want to create their own personal wiki to use for their own organization, project management, or lesson planning outside of the wiki provided by district or school. Resist the urge to control wiki use. These personal explorations allow users to learn more and understand the

wiki much more deeply. Access to these wiki farms also allows employees to become exposed to wikis used in other schools and districts, to network with other educators who have adopted wiki use, and to see a wide variety of uses across classrooms, schools, and districts.

Do get permission to publish images of students and colleagues.
This is a no-brainer for legal reasons—especially when students are involved. While it normally is not necessary to request permission of colleagues, it is always courteous to do so. Some schools have students and staff complete some sort of media release form at the beginning of the school year, while others obtain the release on a case-by-case basis when photos are selected for use. Your school or district may have a specific policy in place that dictates how and when to obtain the release so you should always be aware of those policies before deciding to publish images of students and staff.

Do praise and encourage *any* participation; then, praise and encourage for meaningful participation.
We are human. We all like to receive a "pat on the back" when we participate in ways that add value to the whole. When we receive this kind of acknowledgment, we are encouraged to continue participating because we feel supported, and we feel as if our voice and our effort are valued. Public praise and encouragement may also send an encouraging message to staff members who have been reluctant to use the wiki in their work.

Do insist on real names for username. Don't allow for anonymous edits or comments. Do set a positive, constructive tone early.
Online etiquette is very important because we lose the visual and verbal cues that are present in face-to-face settings. If everyone has not already learned how to communicate effectively in online text environments (for example, through email use), then they will need coaching in order to participate and collaborate in a positive and effective way with others on the team. Experienced users and leaders can model this communication behavior through their own participation. The use of real names helps provide the transparency necessary for safe, positive, and effective online collaboration and it holds people accountable for the content that they create. If privacy is a concern, adopt the common practice of using either first names with last initial only or last names with first initial only.

Do start small and make edits together as a group the first time.
Group mentoring of new technologies can be as effective as one-on-one mentoring, but, of course, this is even more effective if paired with follow-up mentoring for employees who find the wiki challenging. Create a structured

activity where everyone will be allowed the opportunity to create his or her personal profile page together in a meeting. This allows for a nonthreatening introduction to basic wiki use and page editing.

Do promote the use of wiki over email and avoid the temptation to provide information in media other than the wiki.
Gently remind users to share information through the wiki rather than through email. Model the use of wiki for collaboration and the use of email for short, immediate messages that do not require intensive collaborative efforts. Do not provide alternative media or locations for information and content that is available on the wiki. When employees ask where they can find that information, remind them that it is on the wiki. Initially, you may need to send weekly reminders to staff members to let them know what new information has been added to the wiki or to request their contributions to a document or plan that is currently being edited on the wiki. The wiki should become the one-stop shop for all your documentation and information.

Don't take user experience for granted.
Many of your users will not be Web 2.0 savvy. Be willing to accept that some of your employees have yet to accept email as the standard form of written communication across your organization. You cannot expect these employees to welcome another innovation that requires them to learn a new technology. While you should be aware of this, you should also create opportunities for them to use the wiki with some guided practice. These staff members have varied individual reasons for being reluctant to adopt technology in their work, and it will take time to coach them into building regular technology habits.
The Habit Building Guide section of this book can be used by individuals at their own pace or can be use with the entire staff over a semester or a year to help everyone develop or improve their technology habits.

Do let go of the notion that physical presence is the only prerequisite for collaboration and productivity.
These new tools allow for asynchronous collaboration from any place, any time. In the 20th century workplace, employee productivity was measured in seat time much like learning in school. We must accept the fact that we are now able to work from anywhere at any time. This has been mentioned before but it bears repeating: time is a scarce resource in our business, and it is frequently very difficult to coordinate face-to-face meeting times and locations with busy leadership teams who are taking care of the important school and/or district business. Much of our typical brainstorming and collaboration can take place asynchronously thorough wikis and other web-based tools. This

is an uncomfortable shift for some veteran educators who are accustomed to "face time," but it is a not-so-alien concept for more "wired" workers.

Do provide some one-to-one hand-holding and coaching for users who need it.
One-shot workshops on a professional development day are not effective means for helping faculty learn new technology. Recall the Technology Adoption model and understand that you will have some users who will need some one-on-one time to learn how to use the wiki. This works best if done using a "problem solving" method where the one-to-one time is spent using the wiki to solve an immediate communication or collaboration problem. For example, if a teacher needs to collaborate with another teacher on a lesson plan, the coaching session could focus on developing a template wiki page for the lesson plan, and the subsequent coaching sessions could focus on adding information into the template, updating the page, and making revisions as needed.

Do be patient.
It cannot be stated enough that this process takes time. Be patient with the learning curves of the users and be patient with each individual's path and pace in learning.

Getting Started

Each school and district has its own particular culture and the characteristics of this culture will dictate the most successful process for implementing wiki use within the organization. The following step-by-step process is provided only as a general guide and is not intended to be a one-size-fits-all approach to implementation. You are encouraged to reflect on your own school, district, or department to determine the exact first steps for your team. Feel free to share your "recipe" on this book's wiki (http://wikifiedschools.com) with other readers.

Step 1. Decide on use of a wiki hosting service or a stand-alone wiki installed on your servers. Your first step is going to involve deciding which of many options is best for the needs of your organization. In some cases a mixture of free hosting on "wiki farms" and stand-alone software may be the preferred option. Free wiki hosting services, or wiki farms, include Wikispaces.com, PBWorks.com, Google Sites, and WetPaint.com. Wikispaces.com and PBWorks.com also offer paid wiki solutions that offer a very robust set of features comparable to stand-alone software, and they offer discounts

A Closer Look: Shift Happens—Now What?!

You've just watched "Did You Know" or a keynote by David Warlick—or you have just read this book—for the very first time. You feel your heart begin to race as panic sets in as you think: "My school is in no way prepared to help our students learn what they need for work and life in this very different and constantly changing world. What should I do?!"

Too often, the initial response is to look for money to buy more computers. Some education leaders may say "Let's make sure we have laptops in the hands of *every* student! . . . SmartBoards in *every* classroom!" While it is nice to have administrative support for new technology purchases, a technology-purchasing frenzy is simply not the correct response to the realization that our schools are not doing enough to prepare students for their futures. This is about changing adult perspectives and adult behaviors to create student-centered classrooms that exemplify research-based best practices around learning. It is not about buying the latest, greatest, and most expensive tech toys on the market. Expensive technology in the hands of educators who have not made changes to their behaviors and instructional practice are no better than the traditional chalkboard, pencil, and paper. Even worse, expensive technology that the teachers see no use for will end up just collecting dust in a storage room.

The examples are endless: SmartBoards as expensive chalkboards, PowerPoint and media projectors as flashy and expensive overhead transparencies, computers as typewriters and calculators, distance-learning labs that only get used for faculty or team meetings—or worse, as a nice empty room to use during testing week.

So what should we do when we realize that the world has changed for our students? Rather than immediately engage in a technology-purchasing frenzy, take some time to begin discussions on your campus about how to transform your school into a place where teachers see themselves first as *learners* who are invested in improving their instructional practice through reflection and inquiry, and where students are more globally connected in a way that enhances and supports their individual learning. Collaborate with your faculty and staff—your learners—to learn more about how the world has changed, and what that means for our profession.

Locate the early adopters in your district/schools and bring them in to a conversation around change—recruit them to help spread change virally. Leaders may neglect to involve the early-adopters, and this is a mistake. The early adopters can help drive grassroots efforts so that the change is not perceived as another top-down mandate or the next "new thing" that everyone can just ignore. However, early adopters are only part of the solution, which should also include many conversations and professional learning around the implications of these changes and the use of these technologies in our work.

Change adult behaviors and practices first. Change the way you work together, the way you speak with each other. Change your vocabulary. Begin by redefining yourselves as learners rather than educators. Acknowledge that in order to prepare your students for their futures of the 21st century, all learners on your campus must be equally prepared for those futures, and commit to the belief that being "technophobic" or "technology illiterate" is no longer an option for 21st century learners (and after you have redefined yourselves as learners, understand what that means for professional learning on your campus). Be firm about this—it should not be acceptable on your campus for anyone to say "I don't like technology" or "I'm just not very techie. Can you do this for me?" Banish the phrase "Kids these days" from the vocabulary of everyone on your campus. While you are at it, you should also banish the phrase "My teaching methods have always worked and I'm not going to change just because these kids (fill in the blank)."

Do not form a committee to "study this and bring back suggestions for change." Committees take too long and you just do not have time. Change needed to happen yesterday. Do not create a "pilot project"—same reasons for not forming a committee. It takes too long and change needed to happen yesterday. Pilot projects and committees can be useful if the results are used to move the organization forward. Too often pilot projects flounder and go nowhere while committees are formed and their suggestions are ignored by the decision makers. Too often the development of pilots and committees becomes a way for the administrators to say "See, we are taking action" without having to do the hard work of trying to implement deep, cultural change across the organization.

Do not purchase any new technology hardware until you have first ensured that your network is up-to-date and accessible. How many network drops are in each room? Do you have wireless access across your entire campus? Drops in every room and wireless access across the campus are "must-haves" before you start buying anything else!

Give your teachers time to "play" with Web 2.0, to explore the use of blogs, wikis, Twitter, and more for their professional learning before they attempt to use the same tools in the classroom with students. In fact, put a moratorium on classroom use of blogs and wikis for at least four months until teachers have used them weekly for their own learning by reading and writing and connecting with other edublogging educators. Inform all new first-year learners (new teachers) on your campus that their "learning" is just beginning and will never end—and that it certainly did not end upon completion of all degree and certification requirements. Begin all interviews for new hires with "What is the most recent thing that you learned and how did you learn it?"

Understand that all this can and should happen in conjunction with other changes in professional practice such as Professional Learning Communities and Critical Friends Groups, and along with structural changes such as smaller learning communities, varied student grouping strategies, and/or Early College campuses. Transforming your school into a 21st century learning center does not mean that you throw out other initiatives and other research-based best practices.

Campus leaders should model the professional learning use of Web 2.0 tools through transparent blogging and wiki use with the faculty on a weekly basis. Begin putting all your professional knowledge on a wiki (accessible from anywhere—not on the campus intranet) and when your learners ask where they can find certain documents, policies, and so forth, smile and tell them "It's on the wiki!" Give your learners password-protected access to edit the wiki so that knowledge on your campus is collaboratively developed. This is as much about being transparent in your own learning and in your communication and collaborative decision making with all your learners as it is about modeling the use of new tools.

Parents are also very important stakeholders who need to be a part of the conversations and the learning at all stages of the change process. Parents are also adult learners, and we can accomplish so much more in our schools when they are included.

If our students need to be educated for a globally connected workplace rather than educated for factory work (and yes, they do), collaborate with your learners to make system, process, and structural changes so that your school looks, feels, and functions less like a factory and more like a globally connected communications and learning center. Remember that the most important thing is a change in behaviors and practices—a change in pedagogy—not just buying new technology. Finally, when you do make technology purchases—provide support, provide support, provide support—and provide training. Provide

> training that is a model of effective instruction and learning practices. Create cheerleaders who will coach other professional learners and promote continual learning around changes in the world, economics, technology, and workforce trends that have an impact on our work as learning professionals.
>
> This will require a complete rethinking of the way we structure our organizations. In a time of budget constraints, it is difficult for district or school administrators to rethink staffing and time structures that allow for more professional learning time during the school day. But leaders must rethink both staffing and use of time if they hope to change this culture. Asking teachers to do this on their own time is only a band-aid at best. What is needed is leadership by people who understand the emotional and philosophical challenges of deep change and who are prepared to handle those challenges in a way that is respectful of everyone in the system.

on these packages to schools and school districts. Stand-alone software can include purchased packages that come with support or free open-source software that will require on-site staff who are able to install, setup, and support the wiki. Free open-source packages include MediaWiki (used by Wikipedia and familiar to most people), TikiWiki (http://info.tikiwiki.org/tiki-index.php), and PhpWiki (http://phpwiki.sourceforge.net/), to name a few.

You should begin this decision process by deciding which features you need or want to have on your wiki, then conduct research to identify the hosting service or software that meets those needs. A list of resources that will aid you in your research is located in the Recommended Resources section of this book, and on the book wiki (http://wikifiedschools.com). Your selection at this point will dictate your choice of hosting options:

Install the wiki software or "engine" of your choice on your server, which is either your own hardware, or a server that you rent from a web host. In this option you are responsible for and in control of all aspects of installation, maintenance, upgrades, and support.

Create a wiki on any of the free hosting wiki farms. Someone else is generally in control of installation, maintenance, upgrades, and support. You are able to focus on content, organization, business process, and social functions of the wiki.

Step 2. Start with informal, grassroots implementation. Allow early-adopters to start using the wiki in their departments or teams. These users will be the most likely to invest the time and energy to contributing content, organizing the content, and determining the best ways to use the wiki in your school or district when you are ready to scale up. This works best when administrators allow the early-adopters to explore the use of the wiki without too many limitations or guidelines. Restrict the urge to create too much structure and too many templates early on. There will be plenty of time for developing structure and templates as you scale up.

Step 3. Use an action-research method to document best practices specific to your organization and to determine what works and what doesn't work for your school or district. Document your processes as the wiki develops and allow your early-adopters group to develop user guides for your organization. Their experience will prove to be incredibly valuable as you begin to determine what will work best in your work environment. These best practices can even be documented right inside the wiki on a "best practices" page or space within the wiki. Acknowledge these efforts within the group to show support for the use of the wiki.

Document how the use of the wiki has affected productivity, communication, and collaboration. For some users it will not be enough to just say the use of the wiki is encouraged. These users will want to see evidence that the wiki will have a positive impact on their work. Show them data that indicates reduction in emails, meeting time, and use of storage space. Show them data that indicates more effective communication and collaboration. Include qualitative data as well by surveying users throughout the entire implementation to gauge what is working and not working with the adoption of the wiki.

Step 4. Determine focus, structure, and guidelines. Before rolling out to other users, determine a focus for your wiki, decide on any kind of basic structure for content (keeping in mind that this will change as the wiki grows), and develop some basic community guidelines for content creation, editing, and user interactions. You may want to consider including a "How to use this wiki" section on your wikis to help new users navigate and understand the potential uses. Your grassroots group will be valuable in this stage of development and implementation.

It is possible that you may determine you have more than one focus for the wiki, and depending on the size of your organization, you may decide that you need more than one wiki. If this is the case, you should explore options to integrate the wikis so that users have only one sign-in. With stand-alone wiki software this is possible with the creation of "spaces" that are dedicated to specific teams or specific divisions within an organization.

Step 5. Roll out to other users with training, support, and mentoring. A common question is "How do I get people—all people at all levels of skill and comfort with technology—to use the wiki?" There is no simple answer to this question, but as with all technology integration, it involves a combination of training, support or hand-holding, and continual modeling, and coaching. Successful implementation does require a comprehensive approach to supporting and coaching users, and this means that simply conducting a one-shot workshop at the beginning of the year will not work. The implementation of a school or district wiki will require the investment of time for training, support, and mentoring. Your early-adopters can serve as informal mentors for new users, this being an excellent way for follow-up support after initial training.

One important step that will help with integration is to help all users subscribe to the RSS feed of wiki changes via their email accounts. Ideally, RSS feeds should be sent to an RSS feed aggregator, but until users have developed a habit for using an RSS feed aggregator, they will find subscribing to RSS feeds easier by sending the feeds to their email accounts. To keep users from becoming overwhelmed, it may be best to have them subscribe to specific wiki pages rather than subscribing to the feed for all changes to the entire wiki. When any change is made to the page, a notification will be sent to the user's email address and this serves as a handy reminder to the user to check the wiki for changes.

A model support and mentoring program may involve the development of "technology coaches" who are assigned to each campus or within each department in a larger organization. The technology coach may be a formal position dedicated solely to the development of technology integration and skills, or it may be a title given to an employee who assumes this role in addition to his or her regular duties. See A Closer Look: A Model for Campus Technology Coaches section that follows for further information.

Step 6. Nurture, encourage, and celebrate successes and innovative use. The often overlooked step in any technology implementation project is the most important step for "growing" the technology use. Grow your wiki by nurturing and encouraging your users, then take time to recognize success and innovative uses of the wiki. Has someone learned a new way to embed other media or developed an effective way of using wiki pages with teacher teams? Highlight those accomplishments on a "recent news" section of the wiki, and encourage those users to share their accomplishments through a workshop that they can facilitate to teach others what they have learned or developed.

Technology Coach

What is a technology coach and how does this role differ from more traditional technology positions on school campuses? Most schools have some sort of technology support person and some schools are fortunate enough to have multiple positions, each dedicated to either supporting infrastructure and systems or supporting technology integration in classroom instruction.

A survey of job descriptions reveals that these roles are usually responsible for some or all of the following:

- Assist in planning for effective implementation of curriculum to ensure that technology is used effectively to meet student needs.
- Demonstrate on a regular basis the use of technology in the classroom to improve teaching and learning.
- Plan and provide sustained, in-depth professional development for campus staff that focuses on the integration of technology and curriculum.
- Encourage learning activities that take advantage of computer networking capabilities (e.g., using and creating Internet resources).
- Monitor the use of instructional technology to ensure that resources and activities enhance rigorous academic content and the school's mission.
- Make continual improvements in key processes, techniques, and procedures related to the instructional technology program.
- Provide frequent feedback to staff members and administrators regarding instructional technology.
- Continually search for, evaluate, and implement use of new instructional resources including software, websites, and long-distance learning opportunities.

While most job descriptions for instructional technology positions include language similar to the statements here, rarely do these job descriptions include a specific method or model of how this work should be accomplished over the course of one school year to result in increased adult capacity with technology. Additionally, job descriptions rarely describe what competencies are required for the job and what kind of support or training will be available to help the technology integration specialist improve their own skills in supporting teachers.

The model in the section, A Closer Look: A Model for Campus Technology Coaches, is designed to address these gaps and to increase the effectiveness of those individuals who are tasked with improving and increasing technology integration across the school or organization.

Logistics and Use of Specific Wikis

School leaders interested in using wikis in their organizations have several options, including free options, from which to choose. For those who are just beginning to explore wiki use, the easiest way to get started is to create a free

A Closer Look: A Model for Campus Technology Coaches

Technology coaches have responsibilities to:
- Assist in planning for effective classroom instruction that makes use of technology integration best practices.
- Demonstrate and/or coteach on a regular basis to provide a model on the use of technology in the classroom that improves teaching and learning.
- Plan and provide sustained, in-depth, and just-in-time embedded professional development for campus staff that focuses on integration of technology in curriculum, instruction, and professional practices.
- Encourage and support the development of learning activities that take advantage of emerging technologies in learning.
- Monitor the use of instructional technology to ensure that resources and activities enhance rigorous academic content and facilitate the development of appropriate real-world skills.
- Make continual improvements in key process, techniques, and procedures related to the instructional technology program.
- Collaborate with subject area lead teachers to ensure that instructional technology is integrated appropriately in each curriculum area.
- Provide frequent feedback to staff members and administrators regarding instructional technology.
- Continually research, evaluate, and implement use of new instructional resources including software, web resources and distance learning opportunities.

Technology coaches should:
- Be strong instructional leaders who understand and know how to implement research-based effective instructional methods across the curriculum.
- Be familiar with principles of adult learning (andragogy) and understand how to use cognitive coaching as a method for promoting deeper reflection on individual practice.

- Understand and utilize the effective professional development standards set forth by the National Staff Development Council.
- Understand and use an action research method when coaching educators on the use of new technology in the classroom.
- Understand and apply the National Educational Technology Standards for students, teachers and administrators (NETS-S, NETS-T, and NETS-A) developed by the International Society for Technology in Education (ISTE).

Technology coaches will:
- Attend weekly meetings with other campus technology coaches to increase their knowledge and skills in cognitive coaching, andragogy/adult learning, professional development planning and facilitation, and best practices in use of instructional technologies in the classroom.
- Teach one class section to maintain their own instructional skills and to provide a model classroom that other teachers may observe.
- Chair a campuswide technology committee consisting of teachers, administrators, students, and parents focused on collaborative planning, evaluation, and continual improvement of the overall instructional technology program.
- Develop and maintain (in collaboration with the Technology Committee) a comprehensive Instructional Technology Improvement Plan that guides all professional development and hardware/software acquisitions over the course of each year.

In essence, a technology coach's job should be to work themselves out of a job by increasing capacity to the point where everyone is highly skilled in the use of technology and where everyone has become self-directed learners who can coach themselves through the discovery of and implementation of new technologies in their work and in the classroom.

wiki on one of the popular wiki farms such as Wikispaces (http://wikispaces.com), PBWorks (http://PBWorks.com), WetPaint (http://wetpaint.com) and Google Sites (http://sites.google.com). These three wiki-hosting farms and Google Sites are simple to use for beginners and provide adequate functionality for most knowledge management and planning uses on school campuses. A more technical solution is MediaWiki, a free open-source software package that can be installed on a web server. MediaWiki offers a great deal more functionality, but requires more technical expertise to install, maintain, and use. In this chapter we will explore the features of these four options. We will also discuss basics of using wikis along with syntax used to create wiki pages and "wiki etiquette."

Wikispaces (http://wikispaces.com), one of the most widely used wikihosts in education, provides several levels of subscriptions for users. The basic, free level includes Google Adsense ads, but Wikispaces has generously waived this for educational users. PBWorks (http://PBWorks.com) looks and feels very different from Wikispaces, and offers a few different features. WetPaint (http://wetpaint.com) also looks and feels very different from both Wikispaces and PBWorks, but of the three it offers the widest array of site design options for customization. While both Wikispaces and PBWorks allow for free educational wikis that are ad-free, WetPaint does require a paid subscription to remove the Google Ads from the wiki pages. However, all three services offer many of the same basic features, and Wikispaces and PBWorks offer more enterprise-wiki features with a paid subscription.

Wikispaces, PBWorks, and WetPaint offer these basic features:

- Easy to use collaborative page/article creation and editing
- Complete history of revisions and ability to restore pages
- Use of widget for media embedding
- Full content search
- RSS feeds
- Document management and file sharing through image and file uploads
- Discussion or talk pages
- Wiki backups
- Usage statistics
- Use of tags for identifying key content of each page or article
- Security access controls
- Customization features: CSS, URL, page layout and design (limited with free versions)

Google Sites is actually one of the many online Google tools available to anyone with a free Google account. This tool allows for very easy-to-create dynamic websites, but because the websites can be shared and edited among many users, they are essentially very similar to traditional wikis and many educators are starting to use Google Sites as well as the wiki farms listed above. Google Sites offers these features:

- Ability to create full copies of sites, including copying from Google Apps to Sites
- Subscribe by email to changes for individual pages or the entire site
- RSS feeds for Announcements pages, page comments, and recent site activity
- Default page templates (Web page, Announcements, List, File Cabinet)
- Integration with all Google tools and applications
- Revision history for most page types
- Multiple page layout options
- File storage, including version history
- Access to a full library of custom gadgets which can be used to greatly extend the functionality of Google Sites. Users can also build and insert custom gadgets of their own as a way to include content that may otherwise be rejected by the Google Sites editor.
- No ads are displayed

MediaWiki (http://www.mediawiki.org) is the open-source software upon which Wikipedia is built, and therefore MediaWiki will look and feel very familiar to anyone who has used Wikipedia, especially to anyone who has edited a Wikipedia article. I do not recommend MediaWiki to anyone who is just starting out, and who is only interested in exploring the content creation aspect of wiki use. MediaWiki installation and use is much more technical than the free wiki farm options, but it does offer much more functionality than the free wikis.

For the most recently updated information on the services, features, and subscription requirements of the wiki-hosting sites, you should visit each host's website for more information.

BASICS: The Anatomy of a Wiki

Article or Content Page

The article or content page is the page users see when they first visit the wiki or any of the pages of the wiki. This contains the content that is collaboratively created by the users. If users have editing rights, the article or content page can be edited by clicking on the "edit this page" button. Options for managing the page include editing, viewing revisions history, and discussing the content of the page with other users. These options are usually listed in tabs at the top of the page, however, some wikis such as PBWorks and WetPaint locate these options elsewhere on the page.

The process of adding content or editing content on a page is usually done with a basic visual editor much like the editing tools used in Microsoft Word. All wikis allow some markup language, but even novice users can add content or edit content without knowing the markup language. For more information on the markup language, or syntax, of the four wikis discussed in this book, please see the Resources for Successful Wiki Use in this book: PBWorks Syntax; Wikispaces Syntax; WetPaint Syntax; and MediaWiki Syntax.

One word of caution: Wiki pages and articles cannot be edited synchronously. If two or more people are editing a wiki content page at the same time, some of those edits will be lost when both people attempt to save the edits.

Discussion Page

The discussion page allows wiki users to communicate about the content of the page or article with which it is associated. You can think of this as a message board specifically for one article or one page. Each article or page has its own discussion or talk page. On the free wiki farm wikis, the discussion pages resemble traditional message boards on other websites, while on MediaWiki and other open-source packages the discussion page is a blank page open for editing much like the article or content page. Wikispaces and MediaWiki both use the term "discussion" for this page and both place the link as a tab at the top of the page. Google Sites, PBWorks, and WetPaint refer to this feature as "comments" and both locate the "comments" at the bottom of each wiki page.

On MediaWiki or Wikispaces, you go to the discussion page by clicking on the "discussion" tab at the top of your wiki page.

MediaWiki:

After clicking on the tab discussion, messages are posted using a basic WYSIWYG text editor:

How?—Making It Work in Your Organization ◆ 69

Wikispaces:

After clicking on the tab, discussion messages are posted using a standard form similar to those found on common message boards and web forums:

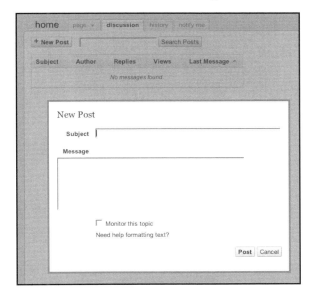

On Google Sites, PBWorks or WetPaint, you go to the comments section by scrolling down to the bottom of the page. There is no need to click on a tab, but users do have to be logged in to leave comments on the page. See

Figure 5.2, a discussion on a PBWorks wiki and Figure 5.3, a discussion on a WetPaint wiki.

Revision History

The history tab contains all the saved revisions of the article or wiki page. Users are able to see the history of revisions, to compare various versions, and to restore previous edits by viewing this tab. Teachers find this feature helpful when tracking student participation on group projects, and all education users will find it helpful to not only be able to see what revisions were made, but to also be able to revert to previous revisions if a page or article becomes corrupted through the editing process. See revision history on a Wikispaces wiki (Figure 5.4); on a PBWorks wiki (Figure 5.5); on a WetPaint wiki (Figure 5.6); and on a MediaWiki (Figure 5.7 on page 72).

FIGURE 5.2

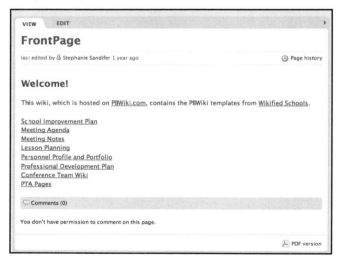

FIGURE 5.3

How?—Making It Work in Your Organization ◆ 71

FIGURE 5.4 Revisions on a Wikispaces wiki

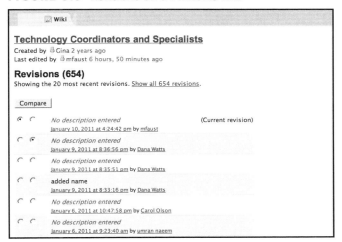

FIGURE 5.5 Revisions on a PBWorks wiki

FIGURE 5.6 Revisions on a WetPaint wiki

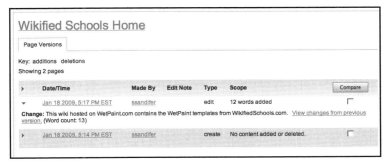

FIGURE 5.7 Revisions on a MediaWiki wiki

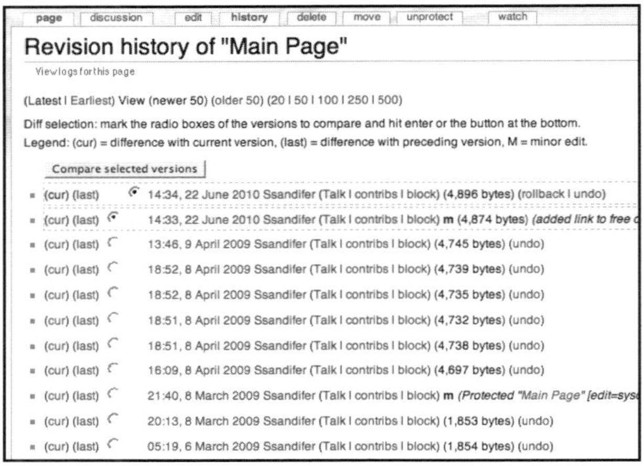

The Importance of Tagging

As you can probably guess, a wiki can become quite large if there are many people contributing articles and edits. Any large database or collection of documents is useless if we are not able to locate the information that is most important to us. As we discussed previously, all wiki articles can be located through the handy Search function but they become even easier to locate when wiki authors and editors make use of "tags."

You can tag each wiki article with keywords. When a user searches on any of the associated keywords, the article will appear in the search even if the term is not included in the article title or content of the page. For example, if you create an article on the Venn diagram that does not include the term "graphic organizer" anywhere in the text, you can tag the page with the keyword "graphic organizer" and when someone else searches the wiki for "graphic organizers," it will show in the search results.

To add tags on a Wikispaces wiki, go to the Manage Wiki section (upper left navigation menu) and select Page. This will give you a list of all of the pages in the wiki. You simply select the checkbox next to the page you want to "tag" and then click on the Edit Tags button above the list of pages. See Figure 5.8.

To add tags on a PBWorks wiki, click on the Edit Page tab and look in the lower right corner of the edit screen to locate the Edit Tags link. This opens a dialogue box where you can add the page tags. See Figure 5.9.

To add tags on a WetPaint wiki, look near the bottom of the page, below "Latest page update" and you will see "Keyword Tags:" You can click on the link that says "(Edit Keyword Tags)" to add the tags for that page. See Figure 5.10.

FIGURE 5.8

FIGURE 5.9

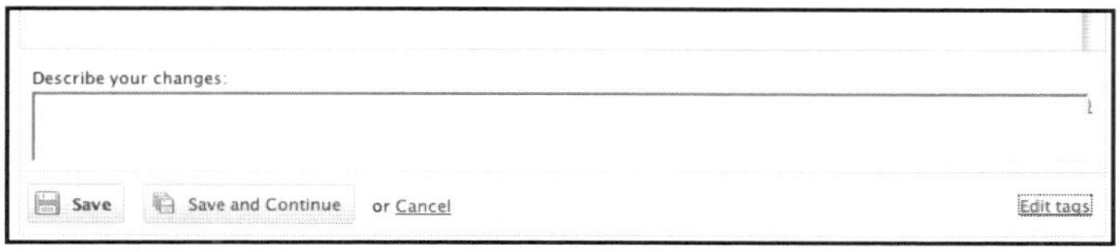

FIGURE 5.10

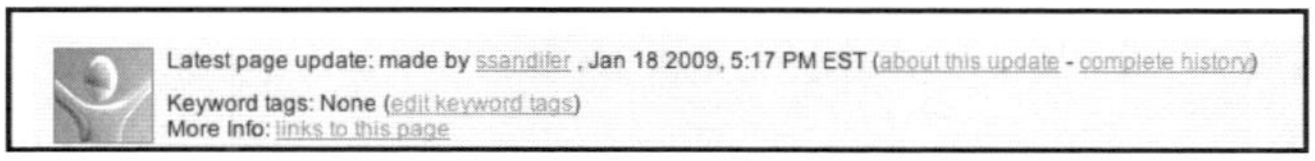

Wikispaces, PBWorks, and WetPaint all use the term "tags" for this feature. However, on MediaWiki this is referred to as "categories" and the process for generating the tags or categories is a bit different because MediaWiki does not provide a field in the editing process. Instead, MediaWiki users create "categories" by entering the following text anywhere into the body of the article or page (usually at or near the bottom): [[category:NameOfCategory]]

At this time, Google Sites does not offer a function for tagging pages, but the use of keywords within the text of each page created will bring those pages up in search even without tags.

Edit or Page Notes

Usually located just above or below the field for tags is another field for entering editing notes. This is a very helpful feature that you should always use when making edits to any page. These notes appear alongside the revision on the history page, and they make it very easy for other users to know instantly the nature of your edit to the page. Examples of notes might be "edited to remove vandalism," "corrected typo," or "updated list of employees."

To add notes on a Wikispaces wiki, simply click the small arrow net to the "Save" button and then select the "Save with Comment" option. See Figure 5.11 on page 74.

FIGURE 5.11

Notes on a PBWorks wiki are entered in the space at the bottom of the Edit page where it says "Describe your changes." See Figure 5.9.

Links

All wiki pages allow editors to create a variety of links anywhere within the content of the page. The kinds of links that are possible include external links to any web page, email links to specific email addresses, links to uploaded content such as image files or documents, and internal links to other wiki pages. Internal links can even be created for pages that do not yet exist. After creating the link and saving the page, clicking on the link to the nonexistent page will trigger the creation of a new blank page that you can easily edit. This is a very handy feature when working on building content in your wiki.

Wiki Etiquette

As with any form of collaboration or communication, in person or online, there are certain general guidelines that individuals must agree upon in order to communicate and collaborate effectively. While these guidelines or etiquette may differ from one culture to another, each is essential for maintaining a sense of order and productive communication.

Here are just a few suggestions for community etiquette guidelines:

- Do not be rude or offensive when posting comments or making edits.
- Do not write "Click here for more information about Collaborative Learning." Instead, write "More info about Collaborative Learning." Avoid doing this for external links as well.
- Do correct typos or content errors.

- Do contribute original content or referenced materials. Follow normal citation and reference rules for academic writing to avoid plagiarizing or violating copyrights and include links to original material that is available online.
- Do use actual dates. For example, write "In August 2009 we implemented a new intervention program" rather than writing "Last August we implemented a new intervention program."
- Do add your signature to comments if applicable and do avoid using first-person references when creating wiki content.
- Do remain objective when adding or creating content. Pros and cons should be included when appropriate.
- Do be bold. Go ahead and create content or edit someone else's work. Remember that this is all about collaboration.
- Do not be offended if someone edits your work. Remember that this is all about collaboration.
- Do include "notes" when you make changes to explain what changes were made and why you made them.
- Do recognize useful content and give praise to constructive work that adds value to the wiki.
- Do help build structure. Allow for collaborative synthesis and structuring of the content by everyone.
- Do follow basic rules of grammar and avoid writing in ALL CAPS, which is considered "shouting" in online communications.
- Do use your own name and not an alias. This helps to build trust among the team and holds everyone accountable for his or her contributions.

You may find it helpful to also review the community guidelines set forth by the Wikipedia community. These guidelines are located at http://en.wikipedia.org/wiki/Wiki_etiquette. However, keep in mind that Wikipedia is an "open wiki" and your etiquette guidelines will most likely be different if you do not have an open wiki.

Finally, always remember the Golden Rule of wikis and be sure to include this on your wiki and when you introduce your staff to the wiki:

If it isn't on the wiki, it is not because it doesn't belong on the wiki . . . It's because YOU haven't added it to the wiki!

Reflection Questions

What are your next steps toward wiki adoption?

_____

_____

_____

What resources do you currently have in place to achieve these next steps?

_____

_____

_____

What resources do you need in order to be successful in your wiki adoption efforts?

_____

_____

_____

6

Sustaining Wikis

While getting started can be daunting, fostering the use of a wiki can be even more challenging. Sustainability requires determined effort and persistence. So how do you know when your wiki has become sustainable and/or an integrated component of your overall technology use across your school or district? What steps can you take if your wiki is still in the beginning or emerging stages to move it toward being more sustainable and institutionalized?

The rubric (see Figure 6.1 on page 78) can help you assess how your wiki is being used in your organization. While the rubric doesn't cover all possible aspects of use, it does cover the most common factors to be considered. Additional suggestions for increasing wiki use follow.

How do we move from *beginning* to *institutionalized*? If you are at the beginning stage, here are strategies to help you move to emerging:

- Look for opportunities to help administrators solve their own problems with the use of a wiki so they can see practical uses.
- Request that district filters not block the free wiki sites such as Wikispaces, PBWiki, Wetpaint, and Google Sites.
- Encourage innovators to continue to use wikis and to document and share how they are using the wiki to increase productivity and improve communication/collaboration.
- Develop activities to engage more users in the process of adding content and editing the wiki.
- Develop a plan to update the wiki more frequently.
- Explore how other media such as videos and Google Docs can support the content being added to the wiki. Try conducting a short survey using a Google Form and embed the form into the wiki.
- Resist urge to restrict user ability to monitor content and to initiate editing, revising, and updating. Inform all users that they each have the right and responsibility to monitor, edit, revise, and update wiki content.

FIGURE 6.1 Wiki Use Rubric: How Are You Currently Using Your Wiki?

Factors to consider	*Beginning*	*Emerging*	*Sustaining*	*Institutionalized*
Administrative support	Administrators are unaware of wiki use or actively disapprove of use, and/or wiki farms such as Wikispaces, PBWiki, and Wetpaint are blocked by district filters.	Administrators approve use of wikis but provide no organized support and do not model use in their own work. Wiki farms are not blocked and most wikis use is limited to the use of free wikis from the wiki farms.	Administrators approve use of wikis and are familiar with how they are being used in the organization. A dedicated wiki installation is in place or organization has contracted with a wiki farm to host a wiki package.	Administrators actively use wiki in their own work, communication, and collaboration with faculty and staff.
Community involvement (in percentages)	Wiki is only used by the very tech-savvy innovators. (10% of staff)	Innovators and early adopters actively use wiki and promote its use. (25-50% of staff)	Wiki use has spread to the early majority. (50-75% of staff)	All stakeholders are actively involved in the use and development of the wiki. (75-100% of staff)
Nature of use	Wiki is used primarily as another website with only one person editing and adding information.	Wiki is used as another website but edited by a few users. Majority of staff is aware of wiki and occasionally use it to find info.	Multiple users collaborate and document work on the wiki	Wiki is used for many collaboration, documentation, and communication purposes.

FIGURE 6.1 Wiki Use Rubric: How Are You Currently Using Your Wiki? *(continued)*

Factors to consider	*Beginning*	*Emerging*	*Sustaining*	*Institutionalized*
Frequency of edits/updates	Wiki is rarely updated more than once or twice per semester/term.	Wiki is updated at least once per month or grading period.	Wiki is updated weekly.	Wiki is updated/edited daily by multiple users.
Integration with other technology and communication/collaboration media	No integration with any other media or systems.	One or two users integrate wiki with other technology.	All users integrate wiki with other technology such as Google Docs, video, etc.	Users fully integrate wiki with other technology such as Google Docs, video, etc. Wiki is also integrated with other district systems such as email or intranet.
Who can edit it? Who makes that decision? How is it made?	Content creation and editing is limited to one person. Content is monitored and moderated by an administrator.	Content creation and editing is limited to a few select people. Content is monitored and moderated by a few select members who have been designated to perform those roles.	Content creation and editing is open to all, but only some people participate in those activities. Content is actively monitored and moderated by a few select members who have been designated to perform those roles, but anyone may make corrections, edits, or may moderate content.	Everyone is able to create content and edit content, and the majority of people have done at least some content creation and editing. Content is monitored and moderated by the whole group on voluntary basis.

If you are at the *emerging* stage, here are strategies to help you move to *sustaining*:

- Coach administrators on using wikis in their own work on a regular basis. Focus on one or two ways initially and consistently remind them to use wikis for those one or two purposes.
- Discuss a dedicated wiki solution with network administrators and conduct research to determine what hosted or installed solution is best for your organization.
- Encourage innovators and early adopters to continue to use wikis and to document and share how they are using the wiki to increase productivity and improve communication/collaboration.
- Look for or create opportunities for early adopters to share what they are doing with the early majority to promote the use of wikis across a wider group of staff.
- Provide structured activities to engage more users in the process of adding content and editing the wiki. Provide weekly reminders to everyone with suggestions on what they may be able to add to the wiki.
- Develop a plan to update the wiki on a weekly basis. Monitor updates and provide gentle reminders/encouragement to promote regular updates.
- Create opportunities for advanced users to share their knowledge of integration with other media (e.g., videos, Google Docs) and provide weekly tips to all to encourage more integration from a wider group of users.
- Coach all users on how to monitor wiki content and how to initiate content editing/revisions/updates. Assure users that permission is not required to do any wiki editing, revisions, or updates.

If you are at the *sustaining* stage, here are strategies to help you move to *institutionalized*:

- Provide opportunities to highlight how administrators are using wikis in their work and how this is improving their work processes.
- Hold town hall meetings with late majority and laggards to determine how and why wiki use is challenging for them and what is preventing them from adopting wiki use in their work.
- Encourage innovative use of the wiki across all business processes, classroom activities, and professional development. Publicly highlight new wiki uses on a regular basis.

- Continue monitoring wiki updates/editing and continue to provide gentle reminders to encourage frequent wiki use. Encourage use of wiki in daily tasks and collaborative activities.
- Discuss with network administrators how proposed wiki solution (hosted or installed) will integrate with other system applications. Seek full integration with email and/or intranet to provide easy access to entire faculty and staff.
- Encourage all users to monitor wiki content and to initiate edits/updates/revisions. Reinforce concept that wiki is owned and operated by everyone.

7

Web 2.0 Tools That Support Wiki Use

The "wikification" of a school or education organization can also involve the use of popular Web 2.0 tools that provide additional avenues for communication and collaboration. Wired educators are using a combination of tools that include wikis, Google Docs, blogs, social networks, and Twitter to just name a few. In this chapter we will quickly review what some of these media are and then we will look at a couple of scenarios to see how all of these can be used together in a comprehensive and powerful communication, collaboration, and learning strategy.

Google Docs

One of the challenges with wiki collaboration is that two or more people cannot simultaneously edit the same wiki page. While two people can be editing the page at the same time, when both people try to save their edits some of the edits are lost as one "save" overwrites the other "save." This is generally not an issue because in most cases wiki editing happens asynchronously. If any particular collaborative project requires synchronous or simultaneous editing of the same document, you may want to consider using Google Docs instead of your wiki. Google Docs is the online text editing application developed by Google. Documents created in Google Docs reside on the Google server, but can be downloaded into documents with various extensions such as MS Word (.doc or .docx), MS Word Rich Text Format (.rtf), or Adobe Systems (.pdf) format.

Another benefit to using Google Docs is that you can format the text as easily as you can in any other word processor, which is helpful if you are collaboratively editing a document that will later be printed out or distributed as a .pdf file.

Additionally, the content from the Google Docs document can easily be copied and pasted into the wiki after the editing is complete. Google Docs works in much the same way as a wiki page where only one document is created and is shared between all users, revisions are tracked, and the document is hosted online rather than residing on a hard drive or traveling around (in multiple versions) on the email server. The biggest difference is that multiple users *can* edit one Google Doc simultaneously with no loss of data or content.

Google Spreadsheets and Forms

Google Spreadsheets and Forms are incredibly valuable for collecting information from users, and like Google Docs, multiple users can edit them simultaneously. As with any Google app, Spreadsheets and Forms can easily be embedded into a wiki page allowing users to interact with the form or data without leaving the wiki page. Some examples include the use of forms for providing feedback, conducting short surveys, and capturing other information directly from users.

Spreadsheets works in much the same way as other spreadsheet applications, allowing the user to track data, perform basic calculations, create multiple sheets in one file, and even embed "objects" such as graphs and charts based on the data. You can also chat in real-time with others who are editing the spreadsheet at the same time and you can attach "notes" to individual cells to provide additional information about the data to other users.

Google Forms allows you to create a web form that can be shared with others to collect data. Forms provide many uses from just collecting basic contact information to doing lengthy surveys. When you create a Google Form, it automatically creates a spreadsheet in Google Spreadsheets. When users complete the web form, the data is entered directly into the spreadsheet immediately. You can see in Figure 7.1 how a Google Form and a portion of the resulting spreadsheet can both be embedded in the same wiki page.

Google Presentations

Google Presentations is Google's version of PowerPoint. Presentations can be created and shared online with all the same benefits of Google Docs,

FIGURE 7.1

February – March Site Visit Sign Up

PAGE   DISCUSSION   HISTORY   NOTIFY ME

We are looking for volunteers to host site visits on their campus on either February 17 or March 31. These are our last two site visits for this year, so if you have not already hosted a site visit please consider volunteering at this time. Please review the chart below to find your preferred date and time if no one has already signed up for that slot. The chart will automatically update as soon as you fill out the form below it, and slots are available on a "first-come, first-served" basis.

Edit This Page

If you do not see your name entered on the matrix after submitting your response, try reloading this page or you can visit the published spreadsheet to verify that your submission has been recorded in the matrix.

February 17 – 9:00 - 11:00 a.m.	February 17 – 1:00 - 3:00 p.m.	March 31 – 9:00 - 11:00 a.m.	March 31 – 1:00 - 3:00 p.m.
			Welch Middle School
		HP Carter Caree Academy	
		Henry Middle	
Grady Middle School			
		B. T. Washington High School	
			Davis High Sc Lanier Middle School
		Pilgrim Academy	
			Pin Oak

February & March 2009 Site Visits

If you are interested in volunteering for one of the remaining site visits, please enter your name below and then enter the name of your campus in the field for the date/time slot that you want. Please refer to the matrix above to see what time slots are still available.

* Required

Name *

February 17 – 9:00 - 11:00 a.m.
Enter the name of your campus if you would like to volunteer for this time slot. Leave blank otherwise.

February 17 – 1:00 - 3:00 p.m.
Enter the name of your campus if you would like to volunteer for this time slot. Leave blank otherwise.

March 31 – 9:00 - 11:00 a.m.
Enter the name of your campus if you would like to volunteer for this time slot. Leave blank otherwise.

March 31 – 1:00 - 3:00 p.m.
Enter the name of your campus if you would like to volunteer for this time slot. Leave blank otherwise.

Submit

Powered by Google Docs

Google Spreadsheets, and Forms. Presentations can be edited synchronously or asynchronously by multiple contributors, viewed online by offsite users in either synchronous or asynchronous situations, embedded into wiki pages and other websites, and can be downloaded as Microsoft PowerPoint files.

FIGURE 7.2

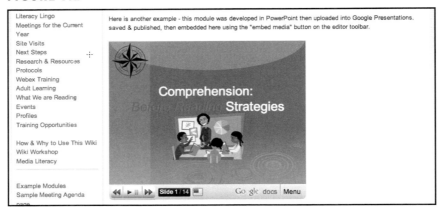

FIGURE 7.3

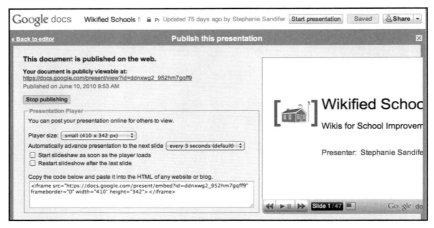

Google Presentations also allows viewers to chat with other synchronous viewers, which creates a live "backchannel" during the presentation. This adds another dimension to the presentation, allowing viewers to discuss with others what they are learning during the presentation.

Any Google Presentation that is embedded into a wiki or other website can be edited from inside Google Presentations and the changes will automatically be reflected in the embedded versions. This is a great feature for any presentations that might be embedded in more than one wiki or website because the edits will only need to be made to the original version, and they will be immediately viewable on all of the embedded versions. See Figure 7.2.

Google Docs, Spreadsheet, Forms, and Presentations all feature the capability of being embedded into a wiki. When one of these files is opened, the

FIGURE 7.4

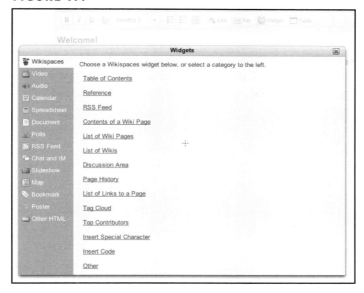

FIGURE 7.5

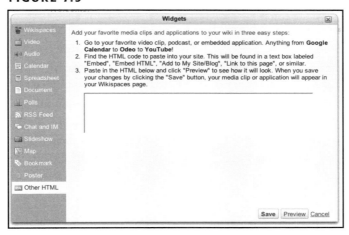

"Sharing" button in the upper right corner of the screen gives users access to the embed code. See Figure 7.3.

This code is entered into a "widget" on the wiki which allows the document, spreadsheet, form, or presentation to appear embedded in the wiki page. The following images show the widget tool used on Wikispaces.com wikis. See Figure 7.4.

By clicking on the "Other HTML" option, the code can be pasted into the HTML box and then saved which automatically embeds the item into the wiki page. See Figure 7.5.

Blogs

Blogs are online journals that provide a space for publishing personal reflections, observations, news, and discussions. Blogs are not online forums and generally do not lend themselves to being a collaboratively authored web resource. Blogs usually only have one author (some have more than one), and other than comments on blog posts, the content is the sole creation of the one author. Blogs are great for providing news, commentary, updates/follow-up on professional development, and promoting group learning activities such as book studies. A blog RSS feed can be embedded onto a wiki page and the RSS feed of the wiki can be included in the blog sidebar with the use of a widget to help link the content from both tools.

Twitter

By now you have probably heard about Twitter in the news, from friends, or from colleagues. Technically speaking, Twitter is a form of blogging referred to as "micro-blogging." Educators who use Twitter frequently refer to it as an "always on, 24-7 help desk and teacher's lounge" where ideas can be shared, links can be posted, and questions can be shared and answered almost instantly. Each Twitter message is limited to 140 characters or less, which promotes brevity and encourages users to write more succinctly while also writing clearly.

Initially, individuals who wanted to use Twitter had some difficulty finding other educators to "follow" and many early users were educators who also had their own traditional blogs. Now there are a variety of online services that allow educators to find other educators who use Twitter, and many of these services allow searching by category as well as by subject or interest area. These services include:

Twibes.com—groups of Twitter users who have a common interest. Some of the larger Twibes include EdTech, elearning, and TeachersOnTwitter.
WeFollow.com—add yourself and then search for others to follow using locations and/or keywords.
MrTweet.com—provides personalized Twitter recommendations based on your own tweets and your current list of people you follow.
Twellow—a directory of public Twitter accounts that can be searched using categories and keywords.

Twitter provides users with widgets that allow Twitter feeds to be embedded in websites, blogs, and wikis. This would allow a school or district that uses a Twitter feed for announcements and public communication to embed the Twitter feed directly onto a wiki page.

Social Networking

Many educators and schools are using social networks to supplement classroom learning, professional development, and professional networking. While some schools do make use of Facebook, other schools and educators are choosing to create closed social networks using Ning.com or to develop their own networks with open-source software.

The benefits of social networking to overall communication, collaboration, and learning include the following:

- Allows participants to make use of network forums and messages to have informal conversations and to learn from and with others in the network.
- Encourages collegiality and shared interests.
- Provides space on individual profile pages for individuals to promote their own ideas, teaching philosophies, and personal or professional interests.

As with all of the tools we have mentioned up to this point, most social networks have RSS feeds which can be embedded in wiki pages, blogs, and websites.

Social Bookmarking

Social bookmarking is very much what it sounds like. Bookmarks are stored online using a service like Delicious.com or Diigo.com and the bookmarks are public so they can be shared with a network of others. You can also see what other people are bookmarking as well as see how many other people have bookmarked the same resources that you have. Educators are making wide use of social bookmarking in their own practice as it is a great tool for personal learning as well as for more social learning in their classrooms. Students benefit from the social aspect of the tools and find them very beneficial to conducting research for individual assignments and group projects.

The two most popular social bookmarking tools, Delicious.com and Diigo.com, allow users to create a widget that can be embedded in a wiki page, blog, or website, and this is a great way to incorporate "link feeds" into a related wiki. One example of this might be a wiki created for art classes which has an embedded link feed containing relevant and useful art museum/gallery websites.

RSS Feed Aggregators

All of these web tools can be overwhelming without some way to manage all of the incoming information, updates, and searches. Perhaps the best way to manage the information is to make use of RSS (Really Simple Syndication), which allows you to pull in only the information you want. You subscribe to RSS feeds for each blog, wiki, news topic, photo gallery or search, or other web content, and the feeds deliver updated content to your RSS feed aggregator or your email inbox as soon as the content is published. Once you begin subscribing to a large body of content, you will probably prefer to not send the content to your email inbox.

The preferred method for subscribing is to use one of the following feed aggregators which provide a variety of ways for organizing and managing your growing subscriptions:

- Google Reader
- Bloglines
- Netvibes
- Photo, Slideshow, and Video Hosting

We all know that learning is enhanced with the use of visuals. This is true online as well as offline, and fortunately there are a variety of free resources online that allow us to incorporate photos and videos into our wikis and blogs. As with everything else, the choice of which tool to use is personal and most of these services provide many of the same features. Many educators use more than one photo-hosting site and many use both YouTube.com and TeacherTube.com to host their videos.

Wikis allow for many of these visual sources to be embedded directly on the wiki page so that viewers do not have to go to an external website to watch the video or the slideshow. However, if a school district does block YouTube.com, those embedded videos will still not be able to be viewed, even when embedded in a wiki page. There are some technical ways to work around this, but in many cases you may still be able to find the same video content on TeacherTube.com or some other online source that is not blocked by the district.

Live Broadcasting and Web Conferencing

In addition to sites that host recorded media, some sites also provide the ability to do live broadcasts and web conferencing. These are great tools for doing webinars or holding districtwide meetings through a web-based application that allows meeting attendees to remain on their own campuses.

Perhaps the most popular broadcasting tool is Ustream.tv, which enables users to host their own live video channel. The stream URL can be shared with others who are able to watch the live stream while also communicating with other live viewers in an attached chat window, and both the video stream and the chat window can be embedded into a wiki page. Educators have used this for streaming of conference sessions, webinars, or holding collaborative meetings online when face-to-face meetings are not possible.

One popular web conferencing tool that allows for a large number of live participants is Elluminate.com. This tool provides audio/video capabilities, a shared whiteboard, screen sharing, and a chat window.

Examples of using these tools are given in Scenarios 1 and 2.

Scenario 1: North School District uses wikis along with a social network to create an "idea marketplace." In the social network forums, group members can publish ideas for improving the school climate, learning environment, instructional program, or other aspects of the school culture and business processes, and other members can vote on those ideas. Ideas that receive a specified number of votes are consider viable and are then posted on individual pages within the wiki for continued collaborative development, testing, and eventual implementation.

Scenario 2: Central School District uses a "wikified approach" to districtwide teams and networks. For monthly principals' meetings, the district publishes the agendas, protocols, and handouts on a wiki, provides space on the wiki for attendees to take notes, and facilitates the meetings through a live broadcast on Ustream.tv. The chat window on Ustream.tv allows attendees to post questions live during the webcast, and notes taken on the wiki can be shared with school leadership teams and/or faculty immediately.

8
Wiki Continued—Edit This Chapter

This book is unfinished. You have explored a variety of uses for wikis in your school environment and seen some examples. The final chapter involves you, the reader, and it does not exist inside this book. The final chapter is a wiki that you can contribute to and it is located online at http://wikifiedschools.com. I invite all readers to visit and join the wiki. In doing so, you can experience firsthand the power of a wiki for collaboration, and you can contribute more ideas for using wikis in your schools. Additionally, the wiki contains other resources such as templates and sample wiki pages in multiple formats for your use.

Resources for Successful Wiki Use

PBWorks Syntax

Type	Syntax	What you see . . .
Internal Link	CamelCaseLink or [Link]	Link
External Link	[http://www.externallink.com]	http://externallink.com
Headlines	! Level 1 !! Level 2 !!! Level 3 !!!! Level 4 !!!!! Level 5 !!!!!! Level 6	Level 1 Level 2 Level 3 Level 4 Level 5 Level 6
Bold Format	**bold**	bold
Italics Format	''italics''	italics
Underline Format	__underline__	underline
Monospace Format	<code>monospace</code>	monospace
Strikethrough Format	-strikethrough-	strikethrough
Superscript Format	super^{script}	superscript
Subscript Format	sub_{script}	subscript
Images	[http://www.URL.com/image.jpg]	Image displayed
Aligning Text	<left>, <center>, <right>	WYSIWYG Left, Right, Center
Text Indentation	Indented block	WYSIWYG indentation
Bulleted Lists	* Bullet #1 * Bullet #2 ** SubBullet #1	Bullet 1 Bullet 2 • Subbullet 1
Numbered Lists	# Number #1 # Number #2	Number #1 Number #2
Definition Lists	<dl>	
Horizontal Rule	----	

Wikispaces Syntax

Type	Syntax	What you see...
Internal Link	[[pagename]] or [[pagename|alias]] or [[spacename:pagename]]	pagename or alias
External Link	[[http://somewhere.else]] or http://somewhere.else or [[http://somewhere.else|text label]]	http://externallink.com or text label
Headlines	= Level 1 = == Level 2 == === Level 3 ===	Level 1 Level 2 Level 3
Bold Format	**bold**	bold
Italics Format	//italics//	italics
Underline Format	__underline__	underline
Monospace Format	{{monospace}}	monospace
Images	[[image:image.jpg]]	Image displayed
Aligning Text	Via editor tool	WYSIWYG Left, Right, Center
Text Indentation	> indent	WYSIWYG indentation
Bulleted Lists	* Bullet 1 * Bullet 2 ** Subbullet 1 * Bullet 3	Bullet 1 Bullet 2 Subbullet 1 Bullet 3
Numbered Lists	# Number #1 # Number #2	Number #1 Number #2
Horizontal Rule	----	
File Link	[[file:name.txt]]	
Tables	|| table cell || table cell || table cell ||	
Table of Contents	[[toc]] or [[toc|flat]]	

WetPaint Syntax

WetPaint sites are edited with an editing toolbar that is completely WYSIWYG (What You See Is What You Get). All of the options on the toolbar are common to most word processing applications and are familiar to most wiki contributors.

MediaWiki Syntax

Type	Syntax	What you see . . .
Internal Link	[[pagename]] or [[pagename|alias]] or [[spacename:pagename]]	pagename or alias
External Link	[[http://somewhere.else]] or http://somewhere.else or [[http://somewhere.else|text label]]	http://externallink.com or text label
Headlines	==level 1== ===level 2=== ====level 3==== =====level 4=====	Level 1 Level 2 Level 3 Level 4
Bold Format	'''bold'''	bold
Italics Format	''italic''	italics
Underline Format	__underline__	underline
Escape wiki markup	<nowiki>no ''markup''</nowiki>	no ''marku''
Images	[[image:image.jpg]]	Image displayed
Aligning Text	Via editor tool	WYSIWYG Left, Right, Center
Text Indentation	:Indent text	indentation
Bulleted Lists	* Bullet 1 * Bullet 2 ** Subbullet 1 * Bullet 3	Bullet 1 Bullet 2 Subbullet 1 Bullet 3
Numbered Lists	# Number #1 # Number #2	Number #1 Number #2
Definition Lists	;Definition :item 1 :item 2	Definition item 1 item 2
Horizontal Rule	----	
File Link	[[file:name.txt]]	name.txt
Tables	|| table cell || table cell || table cell ||	
Table of Contents	[[toc]] or [[toc|flat]]	

Notes: Use of a heading created by single equal signs is discouraged as it appears with the same formatting and size as the page title, which can be confusing.
An article with four or more headings will automatically create a table of contents.
MediaWiki ignores normal line breaks. To start a new paragraph, leave an empty line. You can also start a new line with the HTML tags
or <br/>.

Wiki Adoption Action Plan

Wiki Adoption Action Plan
(available on the wiki: http://wikifiedschools.com)

S.M.A.R.T. Goal:

Strategies:

Resources Needed:

Persons Responsible:

Timeline:

Evaluation:

Note: S.M.A.R.T. Goals: Strategic, Measurable, Aligned, Results-oriented, Time-bound

Wiki Introduction—Sample Workshop Agenda

When?	What?	Why?	How?	What do I need?	Who?
Time for activity	*Name of activity*	*Objectives for activity*	*Methodology detail*	*Materials, supplies, handouts*	*Facilitator(s)*
10 min	Welcome and Overview	To ensure that everyone is set up and on the same page	Guide everyone to the "handouts" on the wiki (the meeting page for today).	Laptops, meeting page on the wiki	
15 min	Anatomy of a Wiki	To develop understanding of the essential components of a wiki	Hands-on overview of the following: Wiki page/article: editing, editing toolbar, tags, notes Navigation & Search function Discussion tab History tab, revisions, reverting, notes Recent Changes (how History can help)		
30 min	Personal Profiles	To practice editing a wiki page/article by creating real content for our wiki.	Everyone will complete their personal profile which can be found on the "Profiles" page (look on the navigation sidebar).	Profiles page template	
15 min	Break	To take care of personal needs and network with other coaches	15 min break		

Resources for Successful Wiki Use ◆ 103

Time for activity	Name of activity	Objectives for activity	Methodology detail	Materials, supplies, handouts	Facilitator(s)
1 hr	Footprints in the Digital Age	To develop better understanding of the importance of developing 21st century technology skills	Text-based discussion: Making Meaning Protocol Step 1: Read "Footprints in the Digital Age" by Will Richardson (from November 2008 ASCD *Educational Leadership* magazine). (20 min) Step 2: On the shared Google doc (link located on agenda in wiki), respond to the question: What do you see? Provide only factual answers without judgment or interpretation. (6 min) Step 3: On the shared Google doc, respond to the question: What questions does this text raise for you? (6 min) Step 4: On the shared Google doc, respond to the question: What is significant about this text? (7 min) Step 5a: Silently read all responses on the Google doc. (5 min) 5b: On the Google doc, respond to the question: What are your thoughts on how this text might influence your work as an educator? (5 min) Step 6: Debrief protocol and Google doc method. (5 min)	Google doc as chart paper Laptops; "Footprints in the Digital Age" article; Making Meaning Protocol	
10 min	Why Wikis Work	To understand why wikis need to be used in our schools (by students and teachers)	Lecture w/slides	Slideshow	

Time for activity	Name of activity	Objectives for activity	Methodology detail	Materials, supplies, handouts	Facilitator(s)
10 min	Wikis & Google Docs	To understand how Google Docs can be used in conjunction with a wiki to enhance professional work	Lecture with examples from our work. A "behind the scenes" look at how Tina, Stephanie, and Paula use both for communication and collaboration with the larger network. Define and explain importance of *asynchronous* vs *synchronous* collaboration.		
15 min	Discussions Tab	To practice using the discussions tab to give feedback or ask questions about a wiki page/article	Everyone will take a few minutes to read some of the other coaches' profiles and then use the "Discussions" tab to give feedback or ask questions about the content of the page.	Profiles pages	
15 min	Wiki Scavenger Hunt	To search the wiki for new documents and new content	Work with a partner to locate the Scavenger Hunt items within the wiki. (Last item—complete the embedded reflections form for today's meeting.)	Wiki Scavenger Hunt page	
5 min	Wrap-up				

Note: Available at https://literacyleads.wikispaces.com/February+17%2C+2009

Wiki Scavenger Hunt

Individually or with a partner, locate the following items within the wiki at https://literacyleads.wikispaces.com/February+17%2C+2009.

Item	Hint
Our Language of Effective Teaching Matrix	an MS Word document created with Dr. Coppenhaver
Literacy Night Out	information about some of the Literacy Night Out events that some schools have hosted this year
ARI Training Modules	archived sessions from the ARI training provided by National Geographic
Literacy Related News Articles	recent news from various sources
Text Rendering Protocol	one of the protocols used in some of our meetings
Rigor Continuum Blank	the blank rigor continuum to be used for on-campus professional development
Today's Reflection Form	embedded form for submitting your reflections from today

Wiki Barn Raising—Personal Profiles

The following is a structured protocol for learning how to use and edit a wiki.

Before The Session

Create a Personal Profile template in your wiki that each user will use when creating their own profile. Template should include space for at least the following basic information: name, school or department, email address, other contact info, and brief bio information.

Create a profiles index page that lists the names of all participants. Make each name a hyperlink to a new page in the wiki. When prompted, use the profile page template to create each page.

Create logins and passwords for all users and distribute these to users beforehand.

Instruct users to bring their own laptops or provide laptops/computers to all of them in a lab setting.

Protocol

1. Using projector and live views of the wiki, direct all users to the profiles index page.
2. Ask each user to click on their own name.
3. Direct users to click on the "Edit" tab and to begin editing their own information.
4. Show users how the editing toolbar allows them to change text formatting, insert images and other media, and include hyperlinks to other websites or other pages in the wiki.
5. Remind users to save their work frequently.

Use this process for other pages that each user can create individually—department pages, classroom pages, personal portfolios or student work galleries, and so on.

Agenda for Short Introduction to Wiki Session

"The simplest thing that could possibly work."
—Ward Cunningham, "father" of the first wiki

Time	Topic	Method	Outcomes	Resources
5 min	Intro and overview of agenda	Lecture	Participants will have an understanding of the overall agenda and how it was developed.	Google Form results; Agenda (online)
20 min	Anatomy of a wiki	Hands-on exploration of the features of a wiki	Participants will develop a better understanding of the features and tools on a wiki.	Printed Wiki Workshop Workbook.doc; Literacy Network Wiki at https://literacyleads.wikispaces.com
15 min	Ideas/examples of using wikis on campus	Lecture	Participants will gain some ideas on how wikis can be used professionally on their campuses or in their regions.	List of examples (see below this agenda) Using wikis in education resources; See http://wikifiedschools.com Templates: http://wikifiedschools.wikispaces.com/

Time	Topic	Method	Outcomes	Resources
30 min	Start your own wiki	Hands-on creation of a personal or professional wiki	Participants will create their own wiki on Wikispaces.	Wikispaces.com—http://wikispaces.com
20 min	Google Docs for better collaboration	Lecture and hands-on creation of a Google Docs account. Collaborative editing of a shared Google Doc. Go to http://docs.google.com and create an account. Use your district email unless you already have a Gmail account.	Participants will create their own Google Docs account and experience synchronous online collaboration with example of a shared document.	Google Docs at http://docs.google.com Google Docs in Plain English video http://www1.teachertube.com/viewVideo.php?video_id=20473&title=Google_Docs; Shared Google Doc at https://docs.google.com/Doc?id=ddnxwg2_825c9b5jk8h&hl=en Google Presentations slideshow at https://docs.google.com/Presentation?docid=ah4zsdj46b66_578cv4x7&hl=en

Links

Literacy Network Wiki (https://literacyleads.wikispaces.com)
Wikispaces (http://wikispaces.com)
Google Docs (http://docs.google.com)
Using wikis in education resources
  (http://wikifiedschools.com/index.php?title=Main_Page)

Wiki Examples

HISD Literacy Network wiki (https://literacyleads.wikispaces.com/)
Wishart Elementary (http://wishart.wikispaces.com/)
St. Francis Xavier Community School
  (http://sfxschool.pbworks.com/w/page/13772188/FrontPage)
Westlake PTO (Wiki used by an Austin, TX, school PTO)
  (http://westlakepto.pbworks.com/w/page/13841128/FrontPage)
ColoradoLearns This wiki is an extension of the Navigator Project, which brought together Colorado policymakers, educators, and other education stakeholders in June 2007 to build a consensus on 21st century learning. (http://coloradolearns.wetpaint.com/)
Brush Schools (http://wiki.brushschools.org/index.php?title=Main_Page)
Principals of the Future (http://principalsoffuture.wetpaint.com/)
  (Blair Peterson) A wiki with resources for principals of technology-rich schools who wish to be visionaries, change agents, modelers, managers and instructional leaders.
Bering Strait School District Collaborative Curriculum
  (http://wiki.bssd.org/index.php/Main_Page)
  This is a standards-based, K–12 curriculum built by BSSD's teachers, students and visitors. The wiki has about 10,000 pages currently, and includes over 2,500 resources uploaded. The curriculum is Open Content and in official use.
And even MORE examples here
  (http://movingforward.wikispaces.com/Wikis)

Wiki Workshop Workbook

Copy and paste the text below into a Google Doc to be shared with all participants. As participants edit this document, they will see all changes reflected in the document immediately and will be able to understand how the synchronous editing works.

Instructions:

Step 1. Choose any of the following questions and take a few minutes to share some of your own notes with everyone who is sharing this document. "Sign" your comment like in the example at the end of this sentence. (FirstName LastName)

Step 2. Choose someone else's note and make a comment on their note. You make a comment by placing your cursor right behind the sentence on which you want to comment and then go to the "Insert" menu and select "Comment." (FirstName LastName 2/15/11 7:55 AM)

Notes

Question	*Notes*
What is a wiki?	
What is not a wiki?	
What is the anatomy of a wiki?	
How can I use a wiki on my campus?	
How do I start my own wiki?	
What are Google Docs?	
How can I use Google Docs?	
How do I set up an account and get started using Google docs?	

Habit Building Guide

Teacher 2.0/Administrator 2.0 One Step at a Time: A Week-by-Week Guide to Building Web 2.0 Habits

In my work with educators who are interested in learning more about Web 2.0, I frequently encounter educators who struggle with lack of time to integrate these tools into their workflow. I often hear "I just can't get into the habit of using these tools," or "I just don't have the time." I do understand these "lack of time" and "habit" issues. Incorporating wikis, blog reading and writing, and social networking into one's workflow does require changed habits. This step-by-step guide is designed to help you develop those habits by spending a little time each week (or each day) focused on one Web 2.0 tool at a time. Each task and reflection builds on previous activities in order to reinforce these new habits, knowledge, and skills.

It may seem odd to publish a step-by-step guide to Web 2.0 in a printed format. Originally, much of the content of this book was online in a Moodle (Learning Management System) and on a wiki, but through my work with educators I found that an online resource just wasn't very helpful for educators who had not yet developed online habits. Too often I received requests from people to remind them where the resource was located because they did not even have an effective bookmarking habit. This guide is not for everyone, but I believe it is necessary for a wide group of educators spanning all age groups. The goal of this guide is to help all educators build a few effective Web 2.0 habits in order to begin working more productively, efficiently, and effectively.

This guide is structured in a very simple manner to help you build these habits by practicing each of them. For each habit building section, you will find the following:

- **Instruction and description of the task.** Some of these are very short and simple, and others require a few different steps in order to complete the task. No task should take more than thirty minutes and some take as little as five minutes to complete.
- **Tips for building this habit.** You can employ these tips hourly, daily, or weekly depending on how rapidly you choose to go through this guide.
- **Notes.** Use this space to take notes as you complete each activity. You may find it helpful to record steps you took, or user logins and password reminders.
- **Reflection questions.** This series of reflection questions is designed to help you think more deeply about each task and to help you

develop ideas or a plan for embedding the habit into your daily practice.
- **Reflection space.** This guide includes space for you to respond to each of the Reflection questions.

Suggestions for Use of This Guide

Some schools and districts have chosen to use this guide with teams of staff members who work together to complete each task on a weekly or biweekly basis during the school year. This is a great way to build a local support group for building these Web 2.0 habits.

Individuals may choose to go through this guide on their own, or to ask a colleague to work through it as well in order to create a "buddy" who will provide support and encouragement through the process.

Regardless of whether you are using this guide on your own, with a partner, or with a larger group of colleagues, you should keep this on your desk in a visible place where you will see it each day. This will help remind you to practice these skills each day, which will lead to the development of new habits.

How do you plan to use this guide?

_____
_____
_____
_____
_____

Getting Started: Computer and Web Browser

Date Started: _____   Date Completed: _____

Before we begin jumping into Web 2.0, we need to make sure our web browser is set up properly to enable us to take full advantage of all that the Web has to offer. Most people still use Microsoft Internet Explorer, but many people who have made the leap to a Web 2.0 lifestyle have started using other browsers like Firefox, SeaMonkey and Google's Chrome browser. All three are useful because of the add-ons that allow better integration with some Web 2.0 services. Regardless of which browser you use, you still need to make some adjustments to help you change your online habits.

Instruction & Task

Step 1. Make Google your homepage. In an upcoming step we are going to create a Google account and set up an iGoogle Homepage, so setting Google as your homepage now is a step in that direction. With iGoogle you can easily incorporate any existing "homepage" content that you already currently use such as your web-based email, local news and weather, and school or district websites.

Step 2. Locate your "Bookmarks Toolbar." This is usually accessible through your Bookmarks menu. We will be adding some bookmarks to this as we develop Web 2.0 habits, and you will need to know where this is and how to edit it before we get started. Editing your Bookmarks Toolbar is usually accessible under the "Editing Bookmarks" option on the Bookmarks menu.

Step 3. In your browser preferences, set your preferences so that new pages will open in a new tab. As pages open, you will see the title of each page listed in a row of tabs at the bottom of your bookmarks bar. Rather than opening new browser windows, you will need to get into the habit of opening new tabs in the same window. This helps with Internet navigation and organization while browsing.

Notes_____

_____

_____

Reflection Questions

Describe your current Web use habits.

_____
_____
_____

What challenges do you anticipate in this process of developing Web 2.0 habits?

_____
_____
_____

Can you name one or two people whom you can rely on for support as you embark on this journey?

_____
_____
_____

What do you hope to accomplish as you go through the activities in this guide?

_____
_____
_____

RSS & Aggregators: Create an Account and Subscribe to the Web

Date Started: _____   Date Completed: _____

Instruction & Task

One of the most powerful aspects of the new Read/Write Web is the ability to subscribe to the RSS feeds of many blogs, news websites, Google searches, and even school district portals—and wikis. RSS stands for "Real Simple Syndication," and it does exactly what it says it will do. It allows you to use a program or website called an "aggregator" to pull information to you in one place rather than your having to go out to multiple websites to search for news and information. An RSS aggregator is one of the essential tools in our efforts to "curate" or filter the vast amount of information and news on the Web.

In order to simplify this task and make it easier for integration with other Web 2.0 tools in later tasks, we are going to focus on Google Reader for our online RSS aggregator. Feel free to explore other aggregators after you become comfortable with Google Reader.

Your task is:

- **Step 1.** Create an account with Google if you do not already have one and then go to http://reader.google.com to set up your Google Reader.
- **Step 2.** Visit the "Getting Started" guide at http://tinyurl.com/GReaderSupport and read through the instructions on getting started with Google Reader.
- **Step 3.** Add the "Subscribe with Google Reader" button to your Bookmarks Toolbar. Go to Google Reader > Setting > Goodies and scroll down to "Subscribe as You Surf." Follow the instructions to place the "Subscribe" button in your bookmarks toolbar.
- **Step 4.** Create an RSS subscription to a news feed. Visit CNN.com at http://www.cnn.com/services/rss/ and navigate to a section of news that you would like to follow. Look for the RSS symbol and click on it.
- **Step 5.** Go to http://supportblogging.com/Links+to+School+Bloggers, look through the list of education blogs and select a few that relate to your interests. Visit each blog and look for the RSS button or a link that says "Subscribe." Click on this and add each blog's feed to your Google Reader feeds.

Step 6. Go to Google Reader and look at how your feeds show in the window.

Wiki Integration Tip: In one of our next tasks, we will learn how we can subscribe to an RSS feed of changes made to our wikis.

Tips for Habit Building

If you choose to use a desktop aggregator, set it to open when you turn on your computer so that it is always accessible.

If you use a web-based aggregator like Google Reader or Bloglines, place the link on your bookmarks toolbar or embed the aggregator into your home page. On a later task we will set up an iGoogle homepage which makes it very easy to embed your Google Reader account on the front page so that it is easily accessible when your browser is open.

Start by trying to check your aggregator once per week. Soon you should find yourself checking it daily. You might want to set aside fifteen minutes each day—morning, afternoon, or evening—to visit your aggregator and catch up on news and blog posts.

Learn to use the "mark all as read" when you find yourself overwhelmed with unread news items. We all have times when we are too busy to check email or other resources, and when this happens the "unread" items will accumulate. You can easily mark all of them as "read" and start with a clean slate with no guilt on your part.

Notes_____

_____

_____

Reflection Questions

How is RSS aggregation different from how you have read news and information on the Web in the past?

_____
_____
_____

What challenges do you anticipate in using an aggregator to pull information to you?

_____
_____
_____

What ideas do you have right now for using RSS feeds and aggregators in your work?

_____
_____
_____

Organizing Your Feeds

Date Started: _____   Date Completed: _____

You will quickly discover that you can subscribe to many different feeds and that the list can be overwhelming unless it has some organization. Fortunately, Google Reader (and most other aggregators) provide ways for you to create folders or categories to help organize your feeds.

Before you begin organizing, start by making a list of all of the different ways you could categorize your feeds. List these in the matrix and then chart some pros and cons to each idea. I've included a couple of examples to help you get started. Use this to make a decision on categorization before you begin creating your folders in your RSS aggregator.

Categorizing Feeds Matrix

Organization Idea	Pros	Cons	Use? (y/n)
By education topics (edtech, ESL, literacy, leadership, etc.)	Very typical and easy to locate specific topics	Where would I place blogs that cover more than one topic?	
By blog author name	Easy to find specific bloggers	Where would I include RSS feeds for news items and nonblog sources? Group blogs?	

Instruction & Task

Step 1. Determine your organization/categorization scheme using the chart above.

Step 2. Go to "Settings" in the upper right-hand corner of the Google Reader screen. Click on the tab that says "Subscriptions."

Step 3. For each RSS feed that you have already subscribed to, change the "Folder" setting on the right-side of the page. When you click on this drop-down button, you will be able to see an option to create a new folder. Click on this and name the folder that you want that item to go into.

Step 4. Do this for each RSS feed in your subscriptions list.

Tips for Habit Building

Create a bookmark or add your Google Reader to your iGoogle homepage as a way to make it visible to you on a daily basis.

If you use the Google Chrome browser, you can install a plugin toolbar that will show you up-to-the-minute data on your Google Reader items such as how many unread posts are currently in your feeds.

Notes_____

_____

_____

Reflection Questions

How did you choose to organize your feeds?

_____

_____

_____

What challenges did you encounter when trying to organize your feeds?

_____

_____

_____

How might this organization aid you in your professional work?

_____

_____

_____

Share Your Subscriptions

Date Started: _____   Date Completed: _____

Instruction & Task

One great feature of Google Reader is the ability to share your RSS subscriptions with others. This is a handy feature for sharing specific RSS feeds related to course topics and campus instructional initiatives. In this task, you will be selecting some RSS feeds to share with your students/teachers.

Step 1. Choose a topic relevant to your current course content/school initiatives.

Step 2. Locate RSS feeds related to that topic. You can also do Google searches in Google News and subscribe to the RSS feed of those news topics.

Step 3. Subcribe to these feeds then use the skills you learned in the previous task to assign those feeds to a new folder titled with the selected topic.

Step 4. Go to "Settings" and click on the "Folders and Tags" tab. Check the box next to your new folder containing the feeds you want to share and then click on the drop-down menu that says "Change sharing. . . ."

Step 5. Change the "sharing" to "public." You will now see options to the right of the folder that include:
- View public page
- Email a link
- Add a clip to your site
- Add a blogroll to your site

For now we will focus on "view public page" by clicking on that option. After you open the new page, you can copy the URL of this page and then paste the URL into an email that you can send out to your students/faculty members.

Wiki Integration Tip: You can generate the RSS feed of these shared items and embed the RSS feed into your wiki page.

Tips for Habit Building

Choose a new topic each month and share some RSS feeds on those topics using the same method described above.

Embed a clip of the shared feeds on your classroom or school wiki and/or website.

Notes_____

_____

_____

Reflection Questions

With whom did you share your RSS feeds? Did they give you any feedback after you shared the feeds with them?

_____

_____

_____

What ideas do you now have for sharing web content through the use of RSS feeds?

_____

_____

_____

Creating Your iGoogle Home Page

Date Started: _____   Date Completed: _____

Instruction & Task

Making iGoogle your homepage in your web browser allows you to create a personalized homepage where you can aggregate all of your essential websites and web tools into one place. You will be creating your own personalized web portal that you customize according to your own professional and personal needs.

Web 2.0 offers us a new and better way to bookmark our web resources, and this method is referred to as "Social Bookmarking." You save your bookmarks to a website that you can access from anywhere on any computer, and you can easily share all of these bookmarks with others.

In this task, we are going to set our Google homepage so that it opens directly to our iGoogle personalized homepage/web portal. We will also add some automatic widgets that will allow us to integrate any other Google tools that we use such as Gmail, Google Docs, and Google Calendar.

Step 1. You should have already done this at the beginning of this workbook. Now you will go into your Preferences and change your default homepage to http://www.google.com/ig.

Step 2. On the right side of your new page you will see a link that says "add stuff . . ." This link takes you to a Google page where you can choose widgets and gadgets to add to your iGoogle homepage. Most users will find it useful to add widgets for weather, calendars, time/clock, and maps.

Step 3. Continue exploring the widgets and gadgets. You can also create new pages for your iGoogle portal so that you can have your top page be your most used widgets and other pages that contain only news RSS feeds or entertainment widgets. For example, your top page may contain only widgets for your Gmail, calendar, maps, weather, Google Docs, and Google Reader.

Tips for Habit Building

The biggest tip for habit building in the use of your iGoogle homepage is to make sure that it is set as your homepage for any and all web browsers that you use on your computer(s). As your homepage, iGoogle will open automatically every time you open your web browser.

Notes_____

_____

_____

Reflection Questions:

How familiar were you with creating personalized homepages before this task?

_____

_____

_____

Which widgets/gadgets did you choose to add first? Why?

_____

_____

_____

How might you expand your use of this tool in the future?

_____

_____

_____

Blog Reading

Date Started: _____   Date Completed: _____

Instruction & Task

We've already touched on blogs just a bit in this book, but now we are going to explore them in a little more depth. The basic layout of most blogs is fairly simple—the content is usually located in the center or the largest column of the page with one or two side columns used for listing other information like blog pages, categories, recent posts, and blogrolls (list of other related blogs).

In this task we are going to explore blogs listed on one popular blogging wiki and learn how to search for blogs online.

Step 1. Visit the http://supportblogging.com website. Navigate to the "List of Bloggers!" page and browse through the list provided on this page. Choose a few of these to explore more closely by visiting their links.

Step 2. As you discover blogs that are relevant to your professional interests, add them to your Google Reader aggregator by using the "Subscribe" button you added to your bookmarks bar in an earlier task.

Tips for Habit Building

Explore the SupportBlogging wiki and pick a few new blogs to read each week. You may want to add a reminder to your calendar.

Add your Google Reader widget to your first page in iGoogle so that you can see any "most recent" blog posts when you open your browser each day.

Notes_____

_____

_____

Reflection Questions

What do you find useful about the structure of the typical blog?

_____
_____
_____

What do you find challenging about the structure of the typical blog?

_____
_____
_____

What topics would you like to learn more about through your blog reading?

_____
_____
_____

How might you and your staff/students benefit from blog reading?

_____
_____
_____

Wikifying Your Work

Date Started: _____   Date Completed: _____

Instruction & Task

This entire book is focused on "wikifying" your work, but in this task we are going to focus on creating a personal wiki to use for a variety of personal/professional purposes. Your personal wiki can initially be a place for you to explore the use of a wiki for content development and to take notes in meetings/professional development. It may eventually evolve into a more public space that houses your professional portfolio or other professional materials that you wish to share with others.

Step 1. Create an account at http://www.wikispaces.com.

Step 2. Go to the following page to create your first wiki. This link allows you to create a free premium wiki exclusively for educators: http://www.wikispaces.com/content/for/teachers.

Step 3. Visit Wikispaces video tutorials site to watch some basic videos that will help you become more familiar with the tools and features of your new wiki: http://www.wikispaces.com/content/wiki-tour.

Step 4. Begin populating your wiki with personal professional materials. You may want to start by creating some of the following pages: notes, lesson plans, meeting agendas, resume/CV, for example.

Tips for Habit Building

Subscribe to the RSS feed for specific wiki pages where you want to keep track of changes. You can subscribe to the RSS feed through your email and receive an email notification each time the page is updated. You can do this by clicking on the "Notify Me" link at the top of the wiki page (next to the Page, Discussion, and History tabs).

Use a wiki page for each meeting that you attend. Open or create a new wiki page at the beginning of each meeting and take your notes directly into the wiki. Create a meeting organization page and place links to each of your meeting notes on that one page.

Notes_____
_____
_____

Reflection Questions

Describe your current collaboration and personal documentation habits?
_____
_____
_____

What challenges do you anticipate in this process of using a wiki?
_____
_____
_____

Can you name one or two people that you can rely on for support as you embark on this journey?
_____
_____
_____

What do you hope to accomplish as you start using wikis in your work?
_____
_____
_____

Glossary

Blog Originally short for "weblog," a blog is just a web page that contains entries in reverse chronological order, with the most recent entry on top. Blogs can be personal online journals or places for engaging others in professional discussions. Readers can "comment" on each post to contribute to the discussion.

Blogroll A list of recommended sites that appears in the sidebar of a blog, these are typically sites that are either on similar topics, sites that the blogger reads regularly, or sites that belong to the blogger's friends or colleagues.

Crowdsourcing The process of tapping into the collective intelligence of a large group of people—usually volunteers—in order to complete tasks or projects. We see examples of crowdsourcing in Wikipedia.com where users voluntarily contribute to articles and on Digg.com where readers contribute, read, and rate news articles (the highest rated rise to the top of the news feed).

Podcast An audio blog which is typically updated weekly or daily. Podcasts are recorded in .mp3 format and may be downloaded to an iPod, or users may listen to podcasts on a desktop computer and other .mp3 players.

RSS Real Simple Syndication is a format for storing online information in a way that makes that information readable by many different kinds of software. Many blogs and web sites feature RSS feeds: a constantly updated version of the site's latest content, in a form that can be read by a newsreader or RSS aggregator.

RSS Aggregator A newsreader gathers the news from multiple blogs or news sites via RSS, allowing readers to access all their news from a single web site or program. Online newsreaders (like Bloglines or Google Reader) are web sites that let you read RSS feeds from within your web browser. Desktop newsreaders download the news to your computer, and let you read your news inside a dedicated software program.

Social bookmarking The collaborative equivalent of storing favorites or bookmarks within a web browser, social book marking services (like del.icio.us or Diigo) let people store their favorite web sites online. Social book-marking services also let people share their favorite web sites with other people, making them an excellent way to discover new sites or colleagues who share your interests.

Social networking Social networking sites help people discover new friends or colleagues by illuminating shared interests, related skills, or a common geographic location. Leading examples include Ning, Facebook, LinkedIn, and MySpace.

Tags Keywords that describe the content of a web site, bookmark, photo, or blog post. You can assign multiple tags to the same online resource, and different people can assign different tags to the same resource.

Wiki A wiki is software that allows users to easily create, edit, and link pages together. Wikis are often used to create collaborative websites and to power community websites. Wikis are used in many businesses to provide affordable and effective intranets and for knowledge management.

Wiki farm Wiki-hosting websites that allow users to create their own wiki without installing software on their own server, wiki farms are excellent options for individuals and for exploring wiki use before committing to a larger wiki installation and implementation project. The most popular wiki farms include Wikispaces (http://wikispaces.com), PBWorks (http://PBWorks.com), and WetPaint (http://wetpaint.com).

Recommended Resources

Books
Disrupting Class: How Disruptive Innovation Will Change the Way the World Learns by Clayton Christensen, Curtis W. Johnson, and Michael B. Horn
Here Comes Everybody: The Power of Organizing Without Organizations by Clay Shirky
Mobilizing Generation 2.0: A Practical Guide to Using Web 2.0 by Ben Rigby
The Wiki Way: Quick Collaboration on the Web by Bo Leuf and Ward Cunningham
Using Wiki in Education by Stewart Mader
Wikinomics: How Mass Collaboration Changes Everything by Don Tapscott and Anthony D. Williams
Wikipatterns by Stewart Mader

Blog Posts
"Your job is to make something happen" by Scott McLeod
(http://www.dangerouslyirrelevant.org/2008/04/make-something.html)
"First Steps Toward Becoming a 21st-Century Educator" by Kim Cofino
(http://mscofino.edublogs.org/2008/04/02/the-21st-century-educator/)
"Disruption or Demand to Learn" by David Warlick
(http://davidwarlick.com/2cents/index.php?s=disruption)
AU: Please check title and url for Purposeful Networking
"Purposeful Networking" by Kate Olsen and Stephanie Sandifer
(http://www.ed421.com/?p=429)
"I'm on a Path—Come Join Me!" by Melanie Holtsman
(http://onceuponateacher.blogspot.com/2008/02/im-on-path-come-join-me.html)
"Don Tapscott Speaks Out on Education" by Vicki Davis
(http://coolcatteacher.blogspot.com/2008/04/don-tapscott-speaks-out-on-education.html (Keynote for Horizon Project 2008)
"9 Principles for Implementation: The Big Shift" by Sheryl Nussbaum-Beach
(http://21stcenturylearning.typepad.com/blog/2008/03/10-principles-f.html)
"ISTE's Refreshed Technology Standards for Students"
(http://www.iste.org/Content/NavigationMenu/NETS/ForStudents/2007Standards/NETS_for_Students_2007.htm)

Wikis & Other Websites
(http://www.classroom20wiki.com/Wikis)
Provides an overview of wikis in education as well as links to many helpful resources and examples.
(http://docs.google.com)
Create your free Google Docs account and begin collaborating on documents, spreadsheets, and presentations. An excellent complement to your school or district wiki.

(http://coollessons.wikispaces.com/Web-based_Communication)
>   Wiki created for a course for educators interested in the use of Web 2.0 tools of blogs and wikis in classrooms. Many helpful resources included.

(http://www.wikiindex.org/index.php?title=Welcome)
>   WikiIndex lists over 3,400 different wikis, along with language, topics and wiki engine.

(http://www.wikipedia.org/wiki/List_of_wikis)
>   Wikipedia's List of Wikis

(http://www.wikimatrix.org)
>   Wikimatrix provides interactive comparisons of wiki packages.

(http://www.springnote.com/en)
>   Springnote is a free wiki-based online notebook used for a wide variety of purposes from writing notes, organization, scheduling, and group projects, among many other possible scenarios.

Wiki Farms (hosting) & Wiki Software:
Wiki Farms Hosting Sites
(http://atwiki.com/@wiki)
>   This free wiki service offers WYSIWIG editing and password protected posts.

(http://www.editthis.info/wiki/Main_Page)
>   EditThis.info allows you a free 25 MB MediaWiki install with unlimited users and pages.

(http://www.etouch.net/products/collaboration/index.html)
>   eTouch SamePage allows teams to work in a collaborative environment on projects, and the free version allows for up to 5 users, 3 projects and 15 pages.

(http://sites.google.com)
>   Google Sites offers free website hosting and development application that works well for wiki creation.

(http://www.littlewiki.com/wiki/)
>   LittleWiki creates a public or private free wiki with WYSIWIG or plain text editors.

(http://PBWorks.com/)
>   PBWorks offers free wikis, but only 10 MB of space. Paid solutions start at $99.50 a year. The service offers password-protected wikis for private or corporate situations.

(http://www.wetpaint.com/)
>   Wetpaint is a free wiki farm that focuses on bringing together the wiki format with blogs and forums. Very much directed towards fan-style sites.

(http://www.wiki-site.com/index.php/Main_Page)
>   Wiki-Site offers free MediaWiki accounts for individuals and groups. Paid accounts get unique domains, access to stats and no advertisements, among other perks.

(http://www.wikidot.com/)
>   Wikidot—300 MB free Wiki for whatever you want.

(http://www.wikispaces.com/)
>   Wikispaces starts at free 2 GB site for friends and families up to paid white label solutions.

(http://www.xwiki.org/xwiki/bin/view/Main/WebHome)
    XWiki offers free solutions as well as paid options for enterprise users. Allows for application development and embedding in pages, along with RSS feeds to keep teams up on changes.

Stand-Alone Wiki Software
(http://sourceforge.net/projects/corendalwiki/)
    Corendal Wiki is a free and open source wiki package directed at corporate users. Slow with updates.
(http://wiki.splitbrain.org/wiki:dokuwiki)
    DokuWiki aims at small companies' documentation needs and offers templating and plug-in support.
(http://www.flexwiki.com/)
    FlexWiki is a free and open source wiki built on the .NET framework.
(http://getwiki.net/-GetWiki)
    GetWiki is a modified version of MediaWiki that provides new features including XML importing.
(http://www.iPBWorks.com/Ipb_Wiki:Integration_Of_Invision_Power_Board_with_MediaWiki)
    IPBWorks offers a system that integrates MediaWiki with Invision Power Boards to make for a whole new wiki experience.
(http://jamwiki.org/)
    JAMWiki is a Java based clone of MediaWiki that uses the same syntax for things such as footnotes, templates and more.
(http://www.mediawiki.org/)
    MediaWiki is a PHP-based, customizable system. Using the same software that powers Wikipedia, it is one of the most popular solutions due to its familiarity.
(http://wiki.mindtouch.com/)
    Mindtouch is a free and open source wiki if you choose to run it on your own host. If you prefer a managed solution for an enterprise install, choose one of various managed solutions.
(http://moinmo.in/)
    MoinMoin has different built-in templates and allows for the support of documents. Its popular framework is used by the likes of the GNOME and Ubuntu sites.
(http://phpwiki.sourceforge.net/)
    PHPWiki is one of the oldest wiki solutions, first appearing in December 1999.
(http://www.pmwiki.org/wiki/PmWiki/PmWiki)
    PmWiki was built more for non-IT people and those that have no wiki background. Easy to change skins and appearance.
(http://info.tikiwiki.org/tiki-index.php)
    TikiWiki is a content management system capable of handling many different jobs, but as the name implies, it favors wikis.
(http://wikkawiki.org/HomePage)
    Wikka Wiki, forked from Wakka Wiki, Wikka has some new features such as support for mind mapping.

References

Black, J. S., & Gregersen, H. (2002). *Leading strategic change: Breaking through the brain barrier*. New York: Prentice Hall.

DuFour, R., & Eaker, R. (1998). *Professional learning communities at work: Best practices for enhancing student achievement*. Bloomington, IN: Solution Tree.

Eaker, R., DuFour, R., & Burnette, R. (2002). *Getting started: Reculturing schools to become professional learning communities*. Bloomington, IN: National Education Service.

Higdon, J. (2005). Teaching, learning, and other uses for wikis in academia. *Campus Technology*. Retrieved from http://campustechnology.com/articles/40629/.

Houston Independent School District. (2008). *Literacy Leads the Way Wiki—Literacy Commitments*. Retrieved March 10, 2011 from https://literacyleads.wikispaces.com/Literacy+Commitments

Howe, J. (2006, June). The rise of crowdsourcing. *Wired*. Retrieved from http://www.wired.com/wired/archive/14.06/crowds.html.

Irvin, J., Meltzer, J., & Dukes, M. (2007). *Taking action on adolescent literacy: An implementation guide for school leaders*. Alexandria, VA: Association for Supervision and Curriculum Development.

Lamb, B. (2004). Wide open spaces: Wikis ready or not. *Educause Review*. 39, 36–48.

Likert, R. (1967). *The human organization*. New York: McGraw-Hill.

Lunenburg, F. C., & Ornstein, A. C. (2004). *Educational administration: Concepts and practices*. Belmont, CA: Thompson/Wadsworth Learning.

Mader, S. (2008). *Wikipatterns: A practical guide to improving productivity and collaboration in your organization*. Indianapolis, IN: Wiley Publishing, Inc.

McGregor, D. (1960). *The human side of enterprise*. New York: McGraw-Hill.

Moore, G. A. (1991). *Crossing the chasm*. New York: Harper Business.

National PTA. (2000). *Building Successful Partnerships: A Guide for Developing Parent and Family Involvement Programs*. Bloomington, IN: National Educational Service.

National School Reform Faculty. (n.d.). *Critical Friends Group FAQs*. Retrieved March 10, 2011 from http://www.nsrfharmony.org/faq.html#1

Reeves, D. (2006). *The learning leader: How to focus school improvement for better results*. Alexandria, VA: Association for Supervision and Curriculum Development.

Richardson, W. (2008). Footprints in the digital age. *Educational Leadership*, November 2008, 16–19.

Richardson, W. (2010). *Blogs, wikis, podcasts and other powerful web tools for classrooms, Edition 3*. Thousand Oaks, CA: Corwin Press.

Senge, P., Cambron-McCabe, N. Lucas, T., Smith, B., Dutton, J. and Kleiner, A. (2000). *Schools that learn. A fifth discipline fieldbook for educators, parents, and everyone who cares about education*. New York: Doubleday/Currency.

Shelley, J. O. (1998, May). Factors that affect the adoption and use of electronic mail by K–12 foreign language educators. *Computers in Human Behavior*, 14(2), 269–285.

Shirky, C. (2008). *Here comes everybody: The power of organizing without organizations.* New York: Penguin Press.

Strauss, W., & Howe, N. (1997). *The fourth turning.* New York: Broadway.

Tapscott, D., & Williams, A. D. (2006). *Wikinomics: How mass collaboration changes everything.* New York: Portfolio Hardcover.

Tapscott, D., & Williams, A. D. (2007, March 27). The wiki workplace. *BusinessWeek Special Report.* Retrieved from http://www.businessweek.com/innovate/content/mar2007/id20070326_237620.htm?chan=search.

Toppo, G. (2009, January 8). Literacy study: 1 in 7 U.S. adults are unable to read this story. *USA Today.* Retrieved from http://www.usatoday.com/news/education/2009-01-08-adult-literacy_N.htm.

Venners, B. (2004, January 19). The simplest thing that could possible work: A conversation with Ward Cunningham, Part V. *Artima Developer.* Retrieved from http://www.artima.com/intv/simplest.html.

U.S. Department of Education. (n.d.). *Literacy FAQs.* Retrieved March 10, 2011 from http://lincs.ed.gov/Faq

U.S. Department of Education, Office of Educational Technology. (2010). *National Education Technology Plan 2010.* Retrieved from http://www.ed.gov/technology/netp-2010

Wagner, T. et al., (2006). *Change leadership: A practical guide to transforming our schools.* San Francisco, CA.: Jossey-Bass.

Westlake High School PTO. (2009). Archived page update from February 19, 2009. Retrieved March 10, 2011 from http://westlakepto.pbworks.com/w/page/13841128/FrontPage?rev=1235080738